Burning the Bracken

Fifteen years of poetry from seren

EDITED BY
AMY WACK

seren

seren
is the book imprint of
Poetry Wales Press Ltd.
First Floor, 2 Wyndham Street
Bridgend, Wales, CF31 1EF

Cataloguing In Publication Data for this book
is available from the British Library

ISBN: 1-85411-168-X

The publisher acknowledges the financial assistance of the
Arts Council of Wales

Original cover art by Lorraine Bewsey.

Printed by: WBC Book Manufacturers, Bridgend.

8

6

CONTENTS

5

11

Introduction

Seren evolved from Poetry Wales Press, begun over his kitchen table with the help and encouragement of poet Dannie Abse, in the early eighties by the then editor of *Poetry Wales* magazine, Cary Archard. Sparked by an initial enthusiasm for poetry, Seren has also begun to publish fiction, drama, history, literary criticism, and the notable *BorderLines* series of biographies. That poetry remains an essential concern is reflected by the shortlisting of two Seren poetry titles for the Arts Council of Wales' Book of the Year awards for 1995. Duncan Bush's excellent collection *Masks* was the eventual winner.

This anthology reflects the genesis of Seren in that it includes selections from authors who began to publish in the late seventies and early eighties, such as Duncan Bush, Sheenagh Pugh, Robert Minhinnick, Christine Evans, Steve Griffiths, Mike Jenkins, Catherine Fisher, Hilary Llewllyn-Williams, Tony Curtis, John Davies, Christopher Meredith, Peter Finch and others who have since gone on to develop distinctive careers. This group could be termed the Third Wave of twentieth-century Anglo-Welsh Literature, the First Wave being writers of the thirties and forties characterized by Dylan Thomas and Idris Davies and represented here by Glyn Jones. The Second Wave appeared in the sixties and featured among others, John Ormond, Ruth Bidgood, Sally Roberts Jones, Leslie Norris, John Tripp, and Tony Conran. This era was marked by editor Meic Stephen's inauguration of *Poetry Wales* magazine, which under successive editors, has continued as a lively and flourishing platform for new poetry. By virtue of having published selected works of certain authors of the first two waves, we are able to include their work here. In some cases, particularly in that of R.S. Thomas, I have only been able to select from one or two volumes that the author has published with Seren, and therefore the selections are not entirely representative of the author's *oeuvre*.

Also here are younger post-Third Wave authors whose work has appeared recently such as Paul Henry, Vuyelwa Carlin, Rose Flint, Lucien Jenkins, Deryn Rees-Jones, Don Rodgers, Barbara Bentley and Frances Sackett. Less accurately 'Anglo-Welsh' than the previous waves, it is perhaps too early to assess their exact place in any critical canon. As most of these have published just one or two collections, they are allocated less space. I am tempted to include Paul Groves, Tim Liardet, and John Powell Ward in this bracket as although they have been around for some time longer, they share stylistic affinities with this group.

Anglo-Welsh remains a problematical term as one tends to hear 'Anglo-Irish' only in negative political contexts and 'Anglo-Scottish' not at all. Indeed Anglo-anything has a decrepit, colonial air. The poems in this anthology, with several exceptions including Newcastle's Desmond Graham and Manchester's Barbara Bentley, are all written in English by people either originating from or working and living in Wales or the Marches. Several authors here also have Welsh backgrounds but have lived for some time in England. Under these flexible rules for inclusion most would qualify to play rugby for Wales, but as to theme, subject and intent, these poems vary as widely as the particular temperaments and inclinations of their authors.

One can, however, point to some broad trends in common. These are apparent even in the most recent work, despite the claims of many that the so-called Anglo-Welsh poets of recent years share a homogenised 'international' style. To some extent the poets of each Wave inescapably share characteristics with the international poetry of their day. This does not mean that they do not retain certain elements particular to their tradition. As a tradition, Anglo-Welsh poetry dates, as Raymond Garlick and Roland Mathias observe in their anthology *Anglo Welsh Poetry 1480-1990*, from the late Middle Ages. It is invariably influenced by the much older traditions of poetry in Welsh with its formalised structures of internal rhyme, cynghanedd, and its famous Bards. The Bard, retainer of a Welsh Lord, was employed to memorise genealogies and to translate the heroic deeds of the Lord into poetry. Welsh language poetry is still a vigorous art and the nineteenth century revival of the eisteddfod, the yearly festival that culminates in the awarding of a 'chair' and a 'crown' to a poet still thrives today.

14

Traces of this great tradition survive in the work of the writers in this anthology. To simplify is to risk inaccuracy and many of these points can be debated in the cantankerous manner of the two old misanthropes in Bryan Aspden's 'Dragons' that opens this book. One can however point to the seriousness in which writers regard their work in Wales and how often the work exists in a sociopolitical and not merely a personal context. Of course this is also an aspect of simply living in a small nation that has been continually subjected, as the historian John Davies points out in his monumental *A History of Wales*, to incursion, to successive waves of invasion. The best example of this is the supreme poet of vitriol, R.S. Thomas. How fiercely his 'Welshman in St. James's Park' clutches his train ticket home! A love of country and despair at its desecration is also the source of the moving elegiac bitterness of John Tripp, the darker ironies of Steve Griffiths and Duncan Bush, as well as the flabbergasted humour of Peter Finch.

Wales shares many of the recessionary trends of parts of Britain in the post-war period and the 'invasions' of recent years are more subtle if no less devastating. Under the conservative onslaught of the Thatcher years, some of these poets responded with outrage; with direct political statement, such as Tony Conran in his 'Elegy for the Welsh Dead in the Falkland Islands.' Others evolved different strategies of expression. Travel was an option and the Anglo-Welsh poets are particularly good at creating a startling sense of otherness, of exile, as in Robert Minhinnick's Technicolour, baroque Brazil in 'Hey Fatman', or in Hilary Llewelyn-Williams' scorching 'Andarax' set in Spain. Tony Curtis' war verses such as 'Soup' are also vivid evocations of European and Far-Eastern conflicts.

Historical poems bring old grievances to light and may be said to shadow the Welsh tradition of tracing genealogies. Catherine Fisher's 'Incident at Conwy' explores a medieval legend of an archer-assassin. Ruth Bidgood's found poem 'Edward Bache Advises His Sister' reveals an incidence of eighteenth-century misogyny. Mike Jenkins imagines a street gathering of protesters in 'Chartist Meeting'. Leslie Norris recounts the bleak fate of a Welsh boxer in 'The Ballad of Billy Rose'. Recent confrontations seem to feature embarrassment over violence and include John Davies' amusingly pushy waiter in 'Border Incident', the train

15

passenger beset by a rugby team in John Powell Ward's 'London Welsh v. Bridgend', and the protagonist of Paul Henry's 'Museum Café', disgusted at the "cream-trousered" bumptious English patrons.

The future is also evoked in several poems, almost always involving nuclear or post-nuclear war catastrophe as in Jean Earle's scary 'Afterwards' where migrating birds arrive to discover an uninhabitable landscape and in Sheenagh Pugh's 'Do you think we'll ever get to see earth, sir?' from her *Earth Studies* sequence in which a teacher hints at the former beauty of a ruined world to the children of its exiled inhabitants. Duncan Bush captures the archetypal fear of doomsday for those born in the nuclear age most movingly in 'The Sunday the Power Went Off'. 'Space Miner' (dedicated to the ex-miner poet, Robert Morgan) by Leslie Norris is intriguing in that it offers its scarred protagonist as an emblem of Wales' recent industrial past and shows the 'pilots' of the future to be shooting off to unknown planets.

A highly-wrought, ironic, allusive and metaphorical language typifies the international poetry of recent years and the post-Third Wave group here share many of these qualities. The complex music of these poems, in some instances, echoes the dense formality of Welsh poetry, particularly in the case of Vuyelwa Carlin, whose distinctive style recalls Hopkins. Tim Liardet's surreal, operatic 'Palimpsest for a Radio Play', Paul Grove's frightening 'The Torturer's Coffee' and Deryn Rees-Jones' eye-opening 'Metamorphoses' all create strange, even perverse worlds out of carefully composed, quirky details. An irreverent oddness is also displayed by Don Rodgers in his ode to a housefly 'Château Lamouche' and by Barbara Bentley's gleeful use of jargon in her 'Telephone Sonnets'. This resort to the peculiar, despite its inherent dramatic interest, is also a response to an increasingly complicated world, one that is, as in Lucien Jenkins' 'Less', shrinking at an alarming rate.

While many poems in this anthology do evidence a contemporary *angst*, there are others that could be said to follow the Welsh tradition of praise poems. The beautiful rural landscapes of Wales, the sometimes harsh lives of farmers and fishermen, inspire Christine Evans, Nigel Jenkins, Hilary Llewelyn-Williams, Joyce Herbert, Kate Johnson and many others.

Character or persona poems abound too and they often serve to praise the survival of an 'average' person as in Sally Roberts-Jones' 'Ellen Owen' and John Ormond's 'My Grandfather and his Apple Tree' and Kathy Miles' 'The Knitter'. Villains and oddballs appear too, such as Paul Groves' chorus line of Eskimo girls in 'Ultima Thule' and Eleanor Cooke's dubious ancestor 'Frederick Durham Scott'. There are also several love poems here such Rose Flint's elaborate 'Brazen Marriage' and Jean Earle's pensive 'Your Aura'.

Every poet that Seren has published is included in this anthology, in alphabetical order by surname of the author. The poems are not necessarily in chronological order of composition. I have generally avoided quoting from sequences or longer, in some cases book-length, poems such as Duncan Bush's *Genre of Silence* and Christine Evans' *Falling Back*. This puts authors whose work is characterised by longer pieces at a slight disadvantage. I hope that interested readers will seek out these fine longer poems. As the idea for this book was inspired by an ebullient remark of Joseph Brodsky's that he didn't see why there wasn't more poetry available in supermarkets, I hope to have succeeded in making this a popular, accessible book. I tried to follow the editorial criteria of Les Murray who, in the Introduction to his selection of Australian poetry mentions that he attempted to choose the best known examples of the author's work and their 'weird' poem. This inculcates responsibility while allowing for just a colourful edge of editorial bias.

Thanks are due to all of the poets represented here with whom it has been my privilege to work with. The Arts Council of Wales deserves much applause for their many years of support. I would also like to thank Cary Archard and family, Sandra Anstey, Michael and Mary Parnell and the recent editors of *Poetry Wales,* Mike Jenkins and Richard Poole. My final salute is to the various Seren staff headed by indispensable Managing Editor Mick Felton and including, over the years, Jean Rees, Ceri Meyrick, Simon Dancey, Claire Collett and Simon Hicks, for their tolerance, inspiration and unsung hard graft.

Amy Wack

Bryan Aspden

Bryan Aspden was born in 1933 in Blackburn, Lancashire. He has lived for thirty years in the Conwy Valley, where he worked as a local government officer until his recent retirement. Author of two Seren collections, the most recent being *Blind Man's Meal*, he is also a fluent Welsh speaker.

Dragons

Their tongues wag over tombstones,
troutstreams and tabernacls —
two old men chewing history's rag
and spitting sugar and vinegar.
It's a near thing
between a knackered pedigree
and a game pitnag
who is the toothiest.

One says:
'The stone roots of our people
grew in these uplands
three thousand years ago',
flaunting his mane
in a helicopter slipstream
or whinnying his pony nose
over a Johnie Walker,
his breath the only fire hazard.

The other chomps the wind
and flashes a red tie
lit by Moscow Mayday:

'Our people? Our first fumbling forefathers?
Celts and coracles? Cobblers:
they didn't know who they were.
Wales hadn't begun
to make itself up.'

'So you say. All you think about's
Rebecca, Scotch cattle,
the Merthyr Martyrs.
What about Dewi's land, Hywel's laws,
our lost parliament our last leader?' —

— 'Saint Sweetface shivering in the sea
loosing a louse from his left testicle.
Leeks and Llewelyn, lovespoons
and Lord Tonypandy
give me the weeping Walias.
Reality's tied to this country
like a tin can rattling its tail.'

Two-handed swords,
Roman eagle rising
over the Marches.
Then the screen fades and the false teeth slide
into their glass of water.
'Tell the tasteless truth: we've given in.
Take it from there.'

A Rum Game

Anchorage, High Winds, the place
where wrought iron dolphins swam
above Harbour View — I crossed them
off my register and went
from the last house in Gannock Park
to the first in Gannock Park West.
In through the double gates, ignoring
the bark and the twitched chain, and trying

to make no noise on the crunchy gravel.
He was standing behind the Mexican
Orange Blossom, with a bedding plant
and a trowel, hoping to finish a border
while the weather kept fine. 'Plaid?'
He shook hands limply with the leaflet I offered.

Tapering, he might have stood
for the flagpole I'd expected on his lawn
though the breath of a Whisky Mac
was all that fluttered in the slight breeze.
'Some good points — the language — half
a Welshman myself,' he huffed, and hawed
a word about the election. Then the garden
he'd bought as a young man thirty years ago
and was lost in now. Neither of us mentioned
the double first in history and drink
who'd have his vote. 'Nice meeting you.
Go that way if you like. It's a rum game.'
I went down a path of cinders, leafmould,
past the groundsel, out through a leaning gate.

News of the Changes

He wears Clarks Movers, his new shoes,
And carries papers to the typing pool,
The section's outmost chamber where
They press him for juice from the centre.
He tells them Colin's here and has made
A Maginot Line of cabinets and trays;
That Maureen's firm and will not move to Legal;
That John Morris the translator
Has changed rooms and taken his kettle.
Sweetened with news they loose him and he goes
Back to his office, where Llew's arrived to toy
With screens and arrows, bilingual signs — all the godwottery
Of order; until the morning's leaked away, and it's time
For sandwiches, and then his lunch hour walk.

He goes past the Pier Pavilion,
The Grand Hotel, The Pier, Happy Valley,
Alex Munro's open-air follies,
The Druids' Circle, the cable car station,
Queen Victoria in her stone pagoda,
Alice, and the White Rabbit, down the steps
To the beach. The tide's coming in. An oystercatcher
Scissors at its edge, and turnstones
Are dabbling their toes in its paper doilies.
As the rocks go under, barnacles
Unbuckle their shells and feed with their feet.
The waves revise their tenses, their soft mutations:
'Ll—', they say coming in; 'L—', going out.

At two o'clock he returns to the Town Hall,
To his desk, and the silt of years clogging his in-tray;
Minutes of sub-committees; dictionaries, forms;
Sonnets; Catalan Grammar; *The Way to Write*.
He's done well from the changes. Is a senior fish
In the local government swim. Others
Are left dry and they complain—
Why should they work the word processor,
Learn floppy discs and software on MO1?
These bubbles of displacement stir
The shallows of the afternoon. He's had enough.
He clocks out early, escapes into the car park.
The Mini that he slipped a disc in's gone.
He drives home in the Mazda past Ffon Tom.

Erw Fawr

Candied fruit is served
on the gateposts this morning.
Candyfloss ravels from a drain
and cars skitter on the road
while I walk Mot past Erw Fawr
that we've watched grow

from a sowing of breezeblocks
to streetlamps on concrete stalks;

what's left of a field,
plasterboard crumbs, cement on ivy,
a hedge in ribbons;
ragwort and yellow rattle
where voles ring their bells: 'Blind, blind!'
as the day owl kerbcrawls by.

You know the spot I mean:
its culture of small dogs, half coconuts,
the nurseryman's favourite escallonia,
'Apple Blossom', lawns with cypress bollards
and merrygorounds of washing? A nice place
to build a greenhouse after Manchester;
where Stan and Connie, Con and Stanley
petition for the planting of trees?

We live across the way. The corner site,
with the bent aerial, the sales-model Citroen Visa;
rhododendrons cringing in the wind,
sick of their diet of limestone chips;
our two children; our two tongues; our two
remaining hens, and their rare eggs.

Barbara Bentley

Barbara Bentley was born in 1950 in Bolton, Lancashire. Educated at Hull and Birmingham Universities, she has recently completed an M.A. in Creative Writing at the University of Glamorgan. She currently works as a lecturer in Leigh, Lancashire. These selections are from her first collection, *Living Next to Leda* (1996).

Eye Test

When he looms before her,
the pin of light of his torch
pricking her pupils, she can see
his strafed skin, so cratered
because he is less than an eyelash away.
There is a glisten that could be orange zest.
She can see his nostrils, at this range
dark and filamented, and feel his breath
warming her cheek like a soft touch.

She wonders how she must seem to him —
whether her blemishes are magnified,
or whether his professional stance
has made him myopic, or blind.

So this transaction is a tacit agreement
that the two parties decline the invitation
of a lover's intimacy.
Unless she misreads his enlarged smile
and the braille of his fingers
smoothing hair behind ears
as he comes in close for the fitting.

from: *The Telephone Sonnets*

Voice Link

Lady, thirty, telephone literate,
(extension, answerphone, mobile and fax,
modem, and so on), with commensurate
voice skills (to conference, tease, or relax),
seeks male, sim, NS, for TLC.
Must have GSOH for pillow talk
in orange or on planet Mercury.
Voice link number 6996. Out. SWALK.

Male, desperately seeking soul fusion
WTLC, though S, tried your VL.
Wow. I'm hooked. Quell my infatuation.
Call up and hear me some time. No hard sell.

M and F souls in vocal harmony,
Unite in fibre optic ecstasy.

Fax

The faxed post slithers through a desktop chink.
FAO The Manager from his wife.
You bastard, it reads. Did you really think
I'd swallow that guff on the phone last night?
Tied up, you said. Too bloody right. Tied up
at some meeting in an en suite, no doubt —
all expenses paid while you're shacked up
with your Personal Assistant. I want out.

The kids send their love. They're strapped in the car.
I should be going. But I'm hanging on
for a phoned through telegram. If you care,
fax us. Fax, damn you. Or we're leaving home.

The document's in a tray marked *Urgent*,
FAO the boss, who's out with a client.

Airing Cupboard

Flimsy as Isadora's scarves, stockings and petticoats
are draped round pipes. On a slatted shelf,
dad's underwear crisps beneath
stiffening shirts. Each ironed crease
is sealed tight, a sharpened edge.

There's no mumness or dadness here —
no Lentheric *Tweed* or builder's sweat —
but something odourless, uncompromising
like the slub of towels hardening
at the bottom of the heap.

Bulbs pulse in dark corners. Compost dusts
the *News of the World.* On the lowest shelf, accessible,
are navy knickers, liberty bodices,
and knee socks interlocked like fists.
My name-taped blouse is starched and virtuous.

I shouldn't pry. Some things are best kept
out of harm's way. The copper tank
scalds like a reprimand as I stretch and grasp
for Dr. White's hidden box. I might be caught
red-handed, fingering his dressings.

Dr. White wears a boil-washed lab coat.
At night his voice, deep and guttural,
comes from the cabinet. Shirts and stockings
dance to his tune. They're fused at hip and sleeve
like a child's paper cut-outs, unfolding.

Ruth Bidgood

Born in 1922 at Seven Sisters in Glamorgan, Ruth Bidgood worked as a coder in Egypt in the Second World War and later on Chambers' Encyclopaedia in London. Now living in Powys, she is a local historian as well as the author of four Seren collections, including 1992's well-received *Selected Poems*. Her recent collection is *The Fluent Moment* (1996).

Kindred

I am still a mile or two
from the source. In spite of myself
I hear the stony flow of the stream
as speech, though not about anything
I know. No bleating, no bird-call;
the only other sound is a breeze
over molinia-grass. It is hard
not to think of a sigh.

On either hand the shallow slope
of the bank steepens, further up,
to a low hill; behind that
rises high land. Nothing seems to grow
for miles but long pale grass
in ankle-turning clumps. My mind
sees little horns of moss on the moors,
cups of lichen on grey rocks,
red-green of whinberry leaves.

Round the next curve of the stream
low broken walls delineate a life

almost beyond my imagining.
Something calls, with a voice
seeming at first as alien
as the stream's, yet inescapable,
and after a while more like
the calling of kindred,
or my own voice echoing
from a far-off encompassing wall.

Spiders

She played the piano sometimes in summer,
when westering sunlight through the open window
gave tarnished candlesticks and dusty curtains
a gentle elegance, so that not to age,
not to fade, would have seemed a lapse of taste.
The hesitant arpeggios, broken trills,
brought great shy listeners from the creepered trellis.
Scuttle and pause, scuttle and pause, came spiders
on tentative delicate legs, to hear the music;
and I, a child, stayed with them, unafraid —
till turning from the yellow keys, one day
she told me of a room where long ago
it had been she who saw the spiders drawn
helpless by threads of music, and listened with them.
Then I felt shut with her into that dream
of endless corridors, rooms within rooms,
mirrors on mirrors compulsively reflected;
while down the corridors, nearer and nearer,
came the great spiders delicately walking.

Sheep in the Hedge

This is no mild and never-never sheep,
but a heavy wild thing, mad with fright,
catapulting at you from a noose of brambles,
hurtling back into worse frenzy of tangles.

Don't imagine you are welcome.
Don't expect gratitude.
That woolly maniac would hate you
if she had any consciousness to spare
from panic. She can see sideways.
There is too much world forcing itself
through slit eyes into her dim brain —
a spiky overpowering pattern of thorns.
Now, worst of all, she suffers the sight of you
(no doubt malevolent), hideously near,
touching her! She wrenches, rips, breaks out,
knocks you into the hedge and is away,
her plump bedraggled body jogging down the road
full-pelt on sticks of legs, pert hooves. You are left
to mop your dripping scratches and stitch up
the tatters of your good intentions.

Tourists

Warner, setting out eagerly from Bath
at five on a lively morning
for the inspiring rigours of Wales
with obliging C......, equipped himself for adventure
with a rusty but respectable spencer
(good enough for North Wales, he said).
The travellers' huge pockets bulged with clothes,
maps, and little comforts; their heads were full
of Ossian, whose horrendous glooms
they were gratified to recognise
one evening on the road to Rhayader
(though Ossian had not prepared them
for the state of the road or the shortage
of bedchambers at the 'Lion').
Romantic tourists, no doubt, perpetual
outsiders, but willing to love,
and finding much 'singular, striking
and indescribable'. They were comic
(embarrassed at being spotted,

with their pedlars' pockets, by fashionable females),
but worked hard for their exaltations,
plodding twenty-five miles to Machynlleth
north over boggy mountains, or stumbling
two hours across rocks to find a guide
to Dôlbadarn ruins. They were uncomplaining
on Snowdon in a thick mist (they drank milk
gratefully, but longed for brandy), and did not grumble
when, at Aberglaslyn, salmon failed to leap
(only two would even try). Who can say
that at the end of August, leaving Chepstow
for flood-tide at the ferry, they were taking
nothing real away, or that their naïve and scholarly wonder
had given nothing in return?

Edward Bache Advises His Sister
a found poem from a letter of 1802, written from Ludlow

Dear Sister,
Although I have no reason
to suspect you of misconduct,
yet my affection and solicitude
will, I hope, excuse these lines
of brotherly advice.
Being visited by men
who profess themselves your admirers,
and not under the protection of your parents,
you are now at the most critical period
in the life of a woman.

Young, inexperienced, unsuspicious,
fond of flattery (as what woman is not),
she too often falls a victim to those worst of men
who, with the aid of oaths, protestations,
and promise of marriage,
seduce her from the paths of virtue,
rob her of her virginity,
and leave her to lament her credulity
in the most abject state of wretchedness,
deserted by her acquaintance,

reviled and scoffed at by her enemies,
a reproach to her friends,
a disgrace to her family,
and, far worse than all of these,
condemned by her own conscience!
The remainder of her life
must be miserable indeed.

If ever you find yourself in danger
of falling into this pit,
think only of the picture I have drawn
and you will shrink with horror
from the dreadful prospect,
and reflect with pleasing terror
on your happy deliverance
from the jaws of a monster so hideous.
Again, dear sister, let me advise you
not to throw yourself away.
You are yet very young,
neither ugly nor deformed,
of a creditable family,
and not entirely destitute of fortune.
Not that I would have you consider yourself
of more consequence than you are,
but I would deter you from doing
that which is beneath you.
Your very affectionate Brother,
Edward Bache.

Stateless

In some nissen-hut of my mind
I have a stacked bed-roll, wooden chair,
suitcase plastered with peeling labels,
and a cheap clock measuring lethargic days.
I have no papers. Sometimes I am offered
forged ones, at too high a price.
Now you come, promising real
identity cards. Forgive me if till they arrive
I think it too early to rejoice.

31

Emu's Egg

Trudging through rain along the windy hill
to pull a snarled-up lamb, whistle the dogs
to their flat-out looping of the ewes,
he nursed the notion of Australia —
heat, space, a chance of more
than his hard-earned Breconshire pittance.
Idea became plan, was told,
marvelled at, acted on. He was best friend
to my old neighbour's grandfather,
turned to him for help — a horse and cart
to Liverpool. Northwards they rattled,
through Builth, Newtown, Welshpool. At Liverpool
came a fraught moment. 'John', he said,
tears not far, 'John, sell the horse and cart,
come with me!' For a moment
that far-off sun shone for his friend too,
coaxing; then it was dimmed
by green damp, more deeply penetrating.
'No', said John, 'I can't, I can't'; turned south
through Welshpool, Newtown, Builth again.

John was dead by the time
a letter came, and an Australian parcel
exotic, unique — an emu's egg,
black, the size (his children said)
of two teacups put together.
It stayed at the farm for years,
then got broken. For a while
they saved the fragments of shell; the story
lasted a little longer. Unlikely transmitter,
I set it down, feeling perhaps for both
brave dreamer and chicken-hearted friend —
one who forced a dream to live, and one
who missed for ever his black two-teacup egg.

Lichen, Cladonia Fimbriata

This little scaly thing,
fibrous lichen, taker of peat-acid
and the rotten juice of dead trees,
grows lowly, slowly, on bog-earth
or the scant soil of crevices,
and holds up to the air its fruit
in tiny fantastic goblets.

Might not this pallid creeping thing,
that needs for food only the sour,
sparse and corrupt, be late to go? —
too small and too tenacious
to be torn off by the dusty wind,
and offering in final celebration
its little tainted chalices?

Earth Tremor

There was a muffled sound, like a train
tunnelling through the hill.
Daffodils in a vase on the table
shuddered for long seconds, long enough
for incredulity to crystalise.

As the small world stabilised
came, illogically, a sense that this
had been something incurred
five minutes, five years ago,
by doing or not doing — a step
not taken, decision bedevilled;
as if it were better to feel guilty
and thankful than know fire-hearted earth
ungovernable, even here.
                              The still daffodils,
never so soft, so crisp, so yellow,
shone, reprieved.

Blue Tit Feeding

Early at the window in starved winter
a little knot of energies, a beaky hunger
fluffed and sleeked, taps, prises
unsucculent scraps of cracked putty,
swallows with a ripple of tiny throat.

Behind it climbs a bleak pale hill
stained with rust of December bracken.
White morning moon is barely seen
on hardly darker sky that seems
opaque, a barrier against pressure
of immensities. Imperceptibly
the chill day flows out to black deeps.

The blue tit pauses in its arid feeding,
flirts a crisp wing. Half-handful of warmth,
it stays for a moment still,
compellingly centre-stage, diminishing
to a backdrop the hill, dull morning sky,
pale echo of moon, black vertiginous
trenches of space-ocean, myriads
of molten and frozen, dying and rising worlds.

Stewart Brown

Stewart Brown was born in Southampton in 1951. He has taught in Jamaica, Nigeria, Barbados and Wales and is currently a lecturer at the Centre of West African Studies, University of Birmingham. Editor of several anthologies of Caribbean literature as well as critical books on Walcott and Brathwaite, he is also a painter and printmaker.

Glad Rags

Rummaging for old snapshots
through a house no longer home
I find Dad's private wardrobe
and discover, like a secret shame,
his stockpile of 'retirement clothes' —

blazers, flannels, shirts and vests,
two pairs of buffed up brogues.
A smart man's hedge against
the grey inflation of his days
into a threadbare dotage.

It is ironic, this late hoarding
to see out a life so blessed
in its bare lack of acquisitions —
no house, no car, and nothing owed.
A life of grime, of beating steel

into a weekly envelope that could,
just, keep his family fed and clothed.

He would not have that pressed
and polished dignity betrayed now
by a pensioned shabbiness

still less leave on that final jaunt
turned out in any but his best.
These furtive, moth-balled glad rags
are his chosen intimates,
his clothes to be seen dead in,
earned and paid for, like the rest.

Springs and Balances

October brings the grasshoppers, suddenly
sprung into our beds, our tea, our hair, like a plague.
Adolescent lizards, wearying of mindless callisthenics
grow paunchy on a few days of such easy meat,
adept themselves at frisky salterello when need be;
eight legged, headless, up to their craws in spoil
they saunter into shade for feast and sleep.
But warily, half eyed: who knows what guise
inevitable retribution may adopt — this compound
once had cats, their smell still haunts its secret corners.

Otherwise the grasshoppers just die, suddenly
in mid flight stoic, stony, pathetically staid maquettes.
They must all die of heart attacks, some main spring overwound.
So they go out as they came in, and lived,
an arbitrary launch into unknown, anarchistic astronauts —
though that implies free will — perhaps more like
those heathen captives of the true god's knights
made reluctant missiles for their blessed mangonels,
the original doodlebugs, screaming as they fell
among awestruck comrades or exploded on to granite battlements.

Their polished corpses litter the yard, suddenly
so much jumble these superbly tailored suits
are tossed away with all the other spent containers,

except for my few *specimens,* laid out on a sheet of paper
like disaster victims waiting to be identified.
They look so stern; this a museum Samuri,
this a folded Bishop taken at his prayers,
and this dun, graveolent beast that must be near a locust
recalling nothing so much, in shape and attitude,
as a Lancaster bomber, standing by, at some wartime aerodrome.

Paralysed to artifice these hollow vessels suddenly
turn metaphors; *being* pared to resemblances.
They remind, remind, of a grandmother struck
through her broad soft heart to a kind of imbecility,
her only and inexorable chant, 'I come I go, I come I go.'
Of the small boy dragged from the sports club pool,
bearded with foam and his lungs black blood,
nor prayers nor respirator could revive him.
Of a history master's virulent aside —
'Statistically one of you morons should have died

before the rest of you get to twenty five.' Suddenly
Paul, in a head on crash, had obliged. And yet
in those few hours flung between absence and infinity
the grasshoppers must have multiplied, bred
another crop of 'lastic legs' as the children call them,
for next year's springs and balances.
And that, maybe, should reassure us, my grandmother's
exasperated chorus merely a statement of fact;
'I come I go, I come I go...' as
October brings the grasshoppers, suddenly.

Calabash Carver, Chaffe

The knife defines the man, gouged
into his trade by an ancient cicatrice.
The gourd rotates. The knife's designs
are old as tradition, unique as his grasp;
there is the sun always, circle or star

37

or ribbon of white, and patterns of notches
alike as the days, among which, deftly,
images of the life his existence defends —
the imperious egret, a suckling calf,
the white bull rampant, pizzle erect

his glans much bigger than his head —
for such gourds are the gifts
you present to a bride, saying;
'May your womb swell ripe as this hemisphere
and your milk run white as its flesh.'

He does not examine his work as he carves,
will bargain and joke without pause,
only stopping to slap hard the belly
of the gourd, to show how she's sound
and worthy of his labour's artless price.

Was-Beetle

'In perfect working order...'
each limb and wing in place,
hairs bristled on the underparts,
this fossil mocks the quick
fantastic creature it portrays
by such stony inactivity.

But what's lost? What fuel
would turn the waiting motors,
set seized bearings on their course?
What lack could be discovered
if this rigoured shell were split?

Was-beetle watches the world emerge,
seems a sweet-meat, pared chocolate
I might devour, suck its answers out
between my teeth, essences
withering tongue like strychnine,
like brilliant scuttling poetry...

Alphobiabet

Anthophobia or *Nurseryman's Nadir;*
fear of rabid dogweed and the snake-head's venom.

Brontophobia or *Thursday's Weather;*
fear of clouds in boxing gloves, of Shango breaking wind.

Claustrophobia or *The Nomad's Energy;*
fear of rattling key-rings and the city's padded cell.

Dendrophobia or *Macbeth's Disease;*
fear of careless lumberjacks and falling leaves.

Equophobia or *The Centaur's Dilemma;*
fear of the senses' rash stampede, or the motorcar's undoing

Faeceophobia or *Kilroy's fever;*
fear of nappy liners and putting one's foot in it.

Gallophobia or *The Snail's Petition;*
fear of gossamer correspondence, of exploding camemberts.

Hydrophobia or *Fire's Heel;*
a titanic fear of icebergs, of living in Wales.

Indophobia or *Raj Rejection;*
fear of dhotis and Far Pavilions.

Jargonophobia or *Sociology's Cancer;*
fear of Art Historians and the Pentagon.

Kissophobia or *The Schoolboy's Terror;*
fear of lipstick and the Judas embrace.

Languophobia or *The Mute's Psychology;*
fear of dictionaries and talking clocks.

Mursophobia or *The Mammoth's Undoing;*
fear of skirting boards and farmers' wives.

Negrophobia or *Powell's Torment;*
fear of Jesse Jackson and the Arsenal football team.

Ophidiophobia or *Eve's Legacy;*
fear of costly handbags and the final rattle.

Paddyophobia or *Paisley's Defence;*
fear of bottled Guinness and Terry Wogan.

Queenophobia or *The Republican's Senility;*
fear of postage stamps and double-headed coins.

Rhymophobia or *Modernism's Allergy;*
fear of greeting cards and poetry circles.

Sitophobia or *Obesity's Dark Sister;*
fear of hamburgers and the carnivorous cabbage.

Thantophobia or *God's Gnawing Doubt;*
fear of angels and the worm's caress.

Europhobia or *John Bull's Last Stand;*
fear of Golden Delicious and UHT.

Virginophobia or *The Whore's Obsession;*
fear of Catholic churches and unread books.

Westernophobia or *Red Indian's Revenge;*
fear of sunsets and the baked beans' lament.

Xenophobia or *Misanthrope's Bedfellow;*
fear of mirrors and manhole covers.

Youthophobia or *The Geriatric's Grimace;*
fear of acne and lollipop men.

Zenophobia or *The Yogi's Rheumatism;*
fear of wind-change and sudden diarrhoea.

Duncan Bush

Duncan Bush was born in 1946 in Cardiff and educated at universities in the U.K. and U.S.A. He is a noted novelist (*Glass Shot*) as well as author of four Seren collections, the most recent being *Masks*, the 1995 Arts Council of Wales' Book of the Year. He currently divides his time between Wales and continental Europe.

Nausea

Summer. Sunday. And carfull after car-
full of the family-dead parking to stare
behind spattered curvatures of dusty
glass in faint, hot reeks of petrol, children's
vomit, car upholstery, unfolding
tubular-frame nylon safari-chairs
on gravel verges stained like garage floors:
stopping for sandwiches, tinned fruit and tea
from thermoses in insulated cups....
The middle-aged, the elderly, the young,
more refugees than ever left Saigon —
from pallid TV screens struck dead by sun
through flowered curtains. The night's dark, film-noir
clarities already draw in them like
an abscess, magnetic North.... A morose
solitary child, too old for his parents,
slumps in the back seat at a lay-by, watches
the cars blur past. They will go further. They
will go as far as you can. They will park
on the promenade, pointing towards the sea.

41

The Sunflower

Bring me the sunflower, so I can transplant it
to my own soil scorched with salt,
and all day long show to the mirrored blues
of sky the golden face of its anxiety.

Dark things turn towards clarity,
exhaust their corporal selves into a flux
of colours: thus, in music. And so, vanishing
becomes the once chance among chances.

Bring me the plant which leads you back
to where blonde transparencies arise
and life is vapourised as spirit;
bring me the sunflower maddened with the light.

(Translated from Montale)

Pneumoconiosis

This is The Dust:

black diamond dust.

I had thirty years in it, boy,
a laughing red mouth
coming up to spit smuts black
into a handkerchief.

But it's had forty years
in me now:
so fine
you could inhale it
through a gag.
I'll die with it now.
It's in me,
like my blued scars.

But I try not to think about it.

I take things pretty easy, these days;
one step at a time.
Especially the stairs.
I try not to think about it.

I saw my own brother: rising,
dying in panic, gasping
worse than a hooked
carp drowning in air.
Every breath was his last
till the last.

I try not to think about it.

                    But
know me by my slow step,
        the occasional little cough, involuntary
and delicate as a consumptive's,

and my lung full of budgerigars.

Hill Farmer, Staring into his Fire

Aye, Ossie Jones can talk of wood, he thought,
weigh ash or beech or sycamore or this
or that, who gets it off a

pickup, block-sawn by the ton. And always he'll
say, smiling as if in trance remembering
some snowy childhood

Christmas-time, Ah, but the finest log of all
to burn is apple — from, I suppose he
means, if he means anything

but common hearsay anyway, that orchard of grey
rough-barked russets, coxes, bramleys,
all older than himself,

that he had cut down for the space to sell to
build a bungalow, forgetting doubtless
in the sweetness of that

smoke the flavour of the apple he can always
buy instead. Me, though, who'd no more
cut a sound

tree down than saw the arm off a young girl, I
think always of the dead wood not
the heartwood: trunks of

rotting birches mossed like stones: the one dry
limb on some old oak, crusted
with lichen stars: that

entire peeled elmtree, white as bone, the wind
brought down one night: stunt
hawthorn from my hedging:

and the alder, the niggardly, prolific alder
that shoots up anywhere, or even likes
the poor-draining places,

and doesn't want to burn, you'd think it stayed
young wood out in the shed, or green or
damp for ever, it shrinks

so slow, burns so reluctant, as if it only bears
the flame from logs beneath it, red
with dying: like that one

uprooted one, and with just a one-man bow-saw —
twig and branch and trunk, aye, stump and
root as well, to keep the land

cleaned up a bit, and with the buzzards coming
right down out of the hills
that year, like ponies —

that I lived a whole, long stubborn winter off.

Living in Real Times

Summer 1993

In Queen St., Cardiff, I halt to watch in a choice
of screens an over of the Trent Bridge test,
Shane Warne looping wristspin in at
some tailender doomed at best to time-serving

till stumps. Between padded-off balls the eye flickers
to the other channel banked in
other sets, headlines unspooling soundless
beyond Curry's window, the newsreader's mouthings:

a street elsewhere foreshortened
by the long lens. Someone running in the tottering
apologetic way the very frightened run,
as if to panic and sprint could only serve

unfailingly to draw the sniper's bullet. Now
someone whom that bullet has already found. He lies
sprawled amid the usual crazed, cradling women
like one adored at last beyond all dreams.

Sarajevo? Mostar? Vukovar?... TV's intimate and
generalising eye makes everywhere somewhere else:
a province of that small, remote country
of which we, famously, know little

still. While post-modernism makes all things
present, all things post-reality (from the intensity
of this particular and very private grief I realise
I saw these shots two hours ago). Again

the street, down which no doubt the dead man too
had run. Past those same bins, the burned-out
truck, between the building's cover and
a water standpipe. Running partway

then throwing his hands up at it all
and falling dead just at that piece of broken kerb....
As he falls over and over again now in the women's
keening, or in some syndicated twenty-second

filmclip replayed over the next day's news.
Night-time, street, streetlight, a chemist's shop,
wrote Alexander Blok as Russia came apart
(that is, the first time round):

whatever you come to, wherever
you go, it all comes down at last
to this. *You'll die, and just as always start
the dance again.* Over and over. And forever

and for ever. No *Amen.* While from the other end,
on another set, Merv Hughes — that moustache
bigger than Nietzsche's — takes the wicket,
a jubilant slip hurling high the catch, fieldsmen

throwing up their hands, the hangdog batsman
turning away, reluctant as a stood-up groom:
live now, sudden, in real time.
And I wait automatically, lingering

to watch them all do it again, in slowmo,
almost missing it the first time,
trained to the instant replay and the freezeframe:
to the destined fact, knowing there's no way out.

Brigitte Bardot in Grangetown

Off Ferry Road, the toilet of a garage where
the mechanics come at lunch to cut the hands' grease
with green Swarfega jelly, glancing once

at themselves in the rust-foxed mirror, and then
go in to eat brought sandwiches and play
pontoon with the soft, soiled pack,

46

three walls of the cubicle sporting the odd grey
newsprint pin-up, some *Kay* or *Tracy*,
alike as playing cards,

and then a whole closed door facing you (if
ever you sat over the stained bowl)
of Bardot as she was at twenty,

and thirty-five, and is now, in her smiling
puppy-fat fifties, still corn-blonde,
and then more of her

again (with one of Ian Rush) out where they eat,
over the workbench's oil and
hacksaw-dust, the clenched vice.

The boy who put all hers up was a six-month
Government trainee. A bit simple, they all thought.
'A headbanger,' the fat one said.

He had a thing about her, the boy, grinning
foolishly, half-proudly, when they kidded him, told him
she was old enough to be

his mother. 'That slag?' the fat one said once.
'Look at her. She's anybody's. Even saving baby seals
all she knows how to do

is lie down with one.' And laughed: soft, smirched face
looking at that photo, then at the one of her
naked, hands raised as if to pin or

loose her hair, the honey-hued still teenage
body, milky Mediterranean behind her, evening.
He left the other week,

the trainee. He didn't finish, he never even came
back for his tools. So now they're
anybody's like the photos:

like, the fat one knows, the photos always are.

A.I.D.S. (The Movie)

Those now-cultish horror movies
from the 'Fifties always were

two-edged to the discerning buff.
In small-town married America

when the alien seed-pods fell
to breed, mutate, occupy human form,

invading *Body Snatchers* spelled
Reds even Inside The Beds, to some;

to others, zombefied neighbours
wandering muzak-eerie shopping malls —

collectivised twin nightmares
where a *Living Dead* walked

almost indistinguishable from
us and their former selves....

Now, past consumerist parable
and Cold War paranoia,

the anxious heart must yearn
back to more hopeful filmic models —

like the old bio-pics re-shown
wet Sunday afternoons in winter,

monochrome *Lives* of the Great
Scientists (Paul Muni as Pasteur,

Montgomery Clift as Freud) — images
of the lone obsessive,

still-uncelebrated
hope of all the ailing world,

stopped at the altar of the cure's
discovery: that private, half-lit

melodrama of a desk lamp nightly
on past dawn.... Oscar nomination,

like the Nobel Prize, are down
as certainties. (But Fleming has

first to have discovered penicillin,
and Mme. Curie — prior to Greer Garson —

radium: the miraculous, hard-won
salvific, glowing in the dark.)

The Sunday the Power Went Off

In a darkening house we sat,
room-light gone, television shrunk
mid-shout to a speck then

nothing, even the old fridge's
whir and periodic
judder stilled,

and saw each other in
flashlit instants while
my five-year-old elder son

counted the sulphur-violet
dimness and I with him:
One. Two. Three. Four. Five:

a second for each year
of his life, and the sum for every
mile as slowly the storm

moved off to a horizon
of rumbles from that sudden
crack in the sky that seemed

right over the roof-ridge
like a rifle-shot amplifying
down a badlands canyon

in movies, the one-off, perfect shot
bringing a man unexpectedly down
forever, though the sunlight

unimpaired, the reel
unfinished, the shocked wildlife
listening a second more then

resuming its tiny business
of survival, even the dead man's
riderless skewbald reaching down to

browse the seeding grass.
Storms now scare me almost more than
my half-scared, half-excited kids,

if only for that first, premonitory
skyquake, distant and dull
as a range of hills or

that dark low cloud like hills
you get at dusk; or for that
faint first flash I know

may any time come before a roar
as of wind and of whirlwind,
finding me sitting

in this same stone house or bending
in the sunlit garden, knowing
instantly under clear air

this wasn't lightning, seeing
wife, sons, sunlight suddenly
reversed, as in a negative,

and simply waiting with them there,
too scared this time to count.

Just a Few Things Daddy Knows About Ice
for Lucas

Starts from water. Starts at zero. Flashes
flow to brittleness. Tightens
as the mercury drops, then cracks
glass. Aspires to the Absolute
Cold of Minus 273
(asymptotic constant like light's speed.
pi's final decimal):
point at which the world
shivers to bits.

More banally:
kills off the dinosaur.
sinks the unsinkable.
Turns the waterfall to stone
and the moisture of your own outbreath
in the air to a tinkle
of falling motes the Russian language
calls the music of the stars.
And clinks in whisky.

Keeps its secret for millenia,
holding the second flood
in the dam, the white continent. Holding
us under the Pole
while weather warms
and the mapped coasts are on the rocks.

Vuyelwa Carlin

Born in 1949 and raised in Africa, Vuyelwa Carlin has spent the last twenty years in the Shropshire countryside, a landscape which deeply influences her work. A prize-winner in both the Cardiff and National poetry competitions, she is the author of two Seren collections, most recently *How We Dream Of The Dead* (1995).

The Topiarist

Since a fierce-quiet child he
has cut this glossy gloom —
it has taken him years
of the old peevish men.

— Now the little rich-
silked boys leap his dwarfy denseness;
and he is a geometrician —
here, his centrepiece,

a star, five points;
— out-radiating, squares
and elegant trapeziums:
he is pale and precise.

Great corner-gaunts of birds,
dark tiers on tiers
of battlements ever-shadow
— fantastical, he is.

In the evenings, close in thick stone,
he shapes boxwood,
orange-yellow prized hardness —
bright, heavy heads.

Lais at Corinth

Demosthenes, I hear — he would not buy repentance
at my so dear price, he said —
so went from Corinth, sunk-eyes,

pewter head; — had he seen me —. My house,
kid white, hangs over the sea: — each waits,
each love, in quaked light, salt bright,

for my songs, my arms, my pleated
thin linen. — Tenderness, I am — send away
the softfoot slave, lave

the cool water fondly. — Had he seen me —
a glimpse, in the town, pale-
wound for the dust, respectful by Aphrodite's

tall hall and shrine; that tameless gloom
whispered by the dark dry women. She, the goddess,
gave me, childish, a beauty

like baby grapes, like rainflowers — now, I fear
her cold large statuary. — My waiting jewelling
dears — death-fierce

I clasp them all, tough-tendril the sunny wall
of their kinder gods, loves. — Demosthenes, old dove-
grey, cruel-strange
not to eye at least my wine and ivory; — seeing, love.

*(Lais — a famous prostitute, assassinated in the temple of Aphrodite
by the women of Corinth in 340 B.C.)*

Medusa Feeds her Pets

Little velvets, I will keep them yet,
— Perhaps they still love me,
Caged on this hidden sandy place
By the tile-blue sea.

When my hair was quiet silk,
And my eyes gentle as green leaves,
I could snug food in my hand
For their mumbled baby-greed,

Take my time. Now they mad,
Poor things, my hissing myriad scalp,
And I flap my hands unstopping
Before these monstrous pulps'

Unblooding gloom. — I must drag now
Cold scales on a stone-starred beach:
But amid my thousand marble guests
The secret softs squeak.

Elizabeth I

Brocaded moths, from all parts
of my land's green profuseness they come; dice
with their plump-bloody
hearts, fledge-soft skins. I have loved

— some; — Midas-wine as I am, lip-strawberries
pulping. — Pearl-
girl I ran with my sharp-eyed nurse
in old closed gardens, kept my eyes

droplet clear for him,
— he hated timid children — frecklebrow,
oaken-fat king fingers
chin-pinching. He strode, rode air

54

like one of his great ships on the sallow quakes — sliced pillars
of God-
hall, green quicks. — Later, grey
gulfing ruby at the long board, physician-

fluttered, bobbed
with lily heads, he watched
with eyes of tallow his young pale,
the boy, his porcelain joy: then, topazed

mud-load, fell. — My little brother's
hair, angel fair,
fell out in his dying days; — little, frail king,
weak eyes potioned every day, old Mother Jack's

nursling. — Amid your ghosts, your myriad
tiny dead, I am your fox-
red; stout boar, your deer grown strong
in dense leaves, father: — queen of these,

the portly swart-cheeks
pushing to the world's blue edge, the small
dogged men wind-grated turning my land, and these,
lovely apricots, milkhands.

from: *Songs of Alfred*

Alfred's Childhood Journey to Rome

I rode with Ealhhere, through ancient greenness,
— summer travellers for a warm December:
under the splashy leaf, in rainbranch chambers,
we covered, fearful of beech-wateriness.

My silent father pressed his poor dark face,
prayed; he was carrying a sorry cumber —
a son, a young man, dead: (I remembered
a horsing in March mud; gleam of fairness).

Monk-murmur where we couched in holy stone:
a cross, hollowed, a joint of finger, saintly,
covered with our dear Lord in ivory —

I went with gold leaf there, forty years on: —
but mostly the endless treeland — how it is rich! —
the snuffly boar-herds, the night-cries, wolvish.

(Water dripping from beech leaves was thought dangerous.)

The Books

Here is sculpture of a thought, mind-mark,
these careful characters, this brilliant stain
flecked with gold; this tenderness of skin: —
here, I touch the mystery, the music

of holy creatures — soul's mould, wisdom's box.
Meticulous makers, cold-fingered in stone,
they shape spirit for us, those Godly men,
our closedness of blind bud to unlock.

They came, stark, to our shores, carrying grace —
bladed with wind clung to our slippery rocks,
built strongholds in our stormy snow and ice:

we have chosen that flint of love, soul-pierce.
— How understand this chiselling of our quicks,
the harsh Dane-sword, but in these hallowed books?

Tony Conran

Born in India in 1931, Tony Conran has lived in Wales since 1939. He has worked as a clerk and a university tutor. Author of many books, his translations are collected in *Welsh Verse* (Seren). In his prize-winning *Blodeuwedd and Other Poems*, the title-poem retells a mediaeval tale from the Mabinogion.

Fern at Ynys Llanddwyn

She crouches on an all-but island,
Rockface bedded in sheets of marram.

Grass stings like a hair shirt
Between muscles of the sand
And the wrenched steel of the wind.

She hides, sniffing the sea-spray.
It is a fern frontier, this coast
Where the grey schist erupts.

She watches the sky, a green girl
Pregnant with epiphytes
From the equatorial trees.

No, that's a daydream. She sniffs salt,
Keeps watch on the Wall.
She is fern on the frontiers of fern.

Though she tries bitterly to
Remember her exile from the jungle,
She could not live there.

Mothering sap swells into sandy groins.
She is native here. She answers
To the breathing of the tide.

Elegy for the Welsh Dead, in the Falkland Islands, 1982

Gẃyr a aeth Gatraeth oedd ffraeth eu llu.
Glasfedd eu hancwyn, a gwenwyn fu.
— *Y Gododdin* (6th century)

(Men went to Catraeth, keen was their company.
They were fed on fresh mead, and it proved poison.)

Men went to Catraeth. The luxury liner
For three weeks feasted them.
They remembered easy ovations,
Our boys, splendid in courage.
For three weeks the albatross roads,
Passwords of dolphin and petrel,
Practised their obedience
Where the killer whales gathered,
Where the monotonous seas yelped.
Though they went to church with their standards
Raw death has them garnished.

Men went to Catraeth. The Malvinas
Of their destiny greeted them strangely.
Instead of affection there was coldness,
Splintering iron and the icy sea,
Mud and the wind's malevolent satire.
They stood nonplussed in the bomb's indictment.

Malcolm Wigley of Connah's Quay. Did his helm
Ride high in the war-line?
Did he drink enough mead for that journey?
The desolated shores of Tegeingl,
Did they pig this steel that destroyed him?
The Dee runs silent beside empty foundries.
The way of the wind and the rain is adamant.

Clifford Elley of Pontypridd. Doubtless he feasted.
He went to Catraeth with a bold heart.
He was used to valleys. The shadow held him.
The staff and the fasces of tribunes betrayed him.
With the oil of our virtue we have anointed
His head, in the presence of foes.

Phillip Sweet of Cwmbach. Was he shy before girls?
He exposes himself now to the hags, the glance
Of the loose-fleshed whores, the deaths
That congregate like gulls on garbage.
His sword flashed in the wastes of nightmare.

Russell Carlisle of Rhuthun. Men of the North
Mourn Rheged's son in the castellated vale.
His nodding charger neighed for the battle.
Uplifted hooves pawed at the lightning.
Now he lies down. Under the air he is dead.

Men went to Catraeth. Of the forty-three
Certainly Tony Jones of Carmarthen was brave.
What did it matter, steel in the heart?
Shrapnel is faithful now. His shroud is frost.

With the dawn the men went. Those forty-three,
Gentlemen all, from the streets and byways of Wales,
Dragons of Aberdare, Denbigh and Neath —
Figment of empire, whore's honour, held them.
Forty-three at Catraeth died for our dregs.

Snowdrops

The snow's gone, the green sinews
Of the world stretch in the woods.
Feeders of light come mewing.
Leaf puts its key to the lock.

From the bud's cornucopia,
From the coracle of the bulb,
The shy ones, the first merchants
Stand with their wares in the mould.

Thirteen Ways of Looking At a Hoover

I

The party suddenly condensed
To the four of us —
Him, and him and her, and me.

I have never seen anger so elegant!
He checkmates them
Lifting their legs
To hoover, ruthlessly, their chair-space.

II

A hoover is like a camel —
It humps itself with provender
And can be trained to spit.

III

One would hardly believe
That even four humans and two cats
Gave so much skin.

Yet, once a week,
The bloated paper intestine of this beast
Has to be emptied of our bits of death.

IV

The difficult slow ease of scything hay —
It is comparable
To her adroitness with its wheels and flex.

V

After many days of toothache
To be grateful for the amnesia
Of a dentist's chair.

And after the long chaos of builders,
Carpenters, electricians,
Destroyers of plaster —

To be sensuously grateful
For the din of a hoover.

VI

In their iron age
The antique hoovers
— All pistons and steel tubes and levers —
In our square-carpeted drawing-rooms
Did not disguise their alienation.

I once turned a corner in Liverpool
And saw, disappearing down a side-street,
A vast, black-leaded steam locomotive,
O-four-O, colossal amid cars.

The antique hoovers, one felt,
Were de-railed like that.

VII

Hoovers would like to be precise.
Their robot souls yearn for clearances
Plus or minus a thousandth of an inch.
Always, by wobble or pile or buffer,
They are betrayed. Your average yard-brush
Is more of a precision instrument!

VIII

The soul of a hoover —
Is it the empty bag
That nothingness blows out like a sail?
Or is it the paradoxical geometry
Of the twisting belt, that burns
Sourly at the ingestion of a tack?

IX

There is a sub-culture of hoovers.
Hoovermen with wiry, terrier moustaches
Poke their heads from dusty limousines
To stop you in the road —

'That new belt I put in —
Has it remedied the fault?
Shall I come to see it?'

Their deft enquiries
Have strict authority over your thoughts.
They carry a king's seal, dispense his justice.

X

Its noise is more sensitive than you'd imagine.
It marks the difference between dusts.

XI

Most of us in a lifetime get to know
One, two, three hoovers. And that is enough.
We think we know the species.

But what of the professionals, the home-helps,
The Rent-a-maids from Hampstead?
Out of the hundreds of hoovers
Their fingers have caressed,
One, two, three stand out
Incomparable.

       As they think of these
Majestic, suave, blond super-hoovers,
Their thighs grow supple with pride,
Their pupils take on the steady gleam
Of an enthusiast, they are fulfilled.

We don't know the half of what hoovers can do.

XII

On what authority you say it I don't know,
But you say, 'The hoover has no Muse'.
Yet from the murk and ashes of our common
Existence, the accumulating death
Of our lives together in this room,
The hoover creates darkness, order, love.
Its wake in the waves of a carpet
Makes lines of growth, furrows a field like a plough.

Could Erato of the laughing eyes, Urania,
Or Melpomene who bore to a slinky river-god
The enticing Sirens, half-girl, half-duck —

Could these *echt*-Muses have ordered it better?

XIII

It's a great virtue in hoovers
You can switch them off.

Eleanor Cooke

Born in 1937 in Yorkshire and educated at Birmingham University, Eleanor Cooke now lives near Chester. A creative writing tutor, lecturer and broadcaster, her most recent collection is *Secret Files* (Cape). Her Seren volume is *A Kind of Memory*.

Walking In

The white house
is where it always was in the dream;
the road behind
twisting into its own double bend.
But I am coming from the other side,
walking towards myself,
still out of sight.

I stare at the reflection of the dream
uncurling itself from sleep, sitting
up in its coffin,
easing into motion.
A stone in the wall
freezes into a wrinkled apprehension;
the road cracks into widening black veins.

I back off, turn,
afraid to glance over my shoulder
to where, behind,
someone who looks like me is striding
out, passing the white house,
closing the gap.

On finding a stage photograph of Frederick Durham Scott

The photograph is of my grandfather.
He does not look our way. The camera,
(propped up behind the curtain, in the wings),
has caught him as he smiled over the footlights.
The spots shining into his eyes reveal
handsome proportions, — maybe a touch flamboyant —
like the handwriting flourished across the darkness
that surrounds the figure: 'With best wishes':
underneath is scrawled the name of a stranger:
in brackets, 'Fred'. On the back, he writes
explaining that he doesn't use his real
name on the Halls. He looks fatter than I
imagined he would be. A man who leaves
his dying wife to tread the boards, ought
to be slender, face lit by a blend of grief,
remorse, resolve — or so it seemed to me.
Romantic, anyway: not plump and smooth,
without a hint of pain. Here is a face
that never saw the gap he left behind
filling with anger, hate — God knows what else.

Perhaps I do him an injustice.
In a three-quarter face it is so hard
to tell. If he had only turned
into the eye of the lens — if only he
had looked, this once, in our direction.

Out of Season

The ground is uneven.
My father's polished shoes
perform amazing feats. He
tipples over shock-headed
clumps of dead grass,
tight-ropes cow-tracks.

His glasses
flash-back mirrored light
to sunburst celandines.
A glance cork-screws him
out of the perpendicular:
he says, 'Buttercups!'
louder than necessary,
and sits on a fallen tree.
He stares at his hands,
turning them slowly under his gaze.
At his feet,
an anger of spiders
rattles
through the dry thatch.

Ellen, Waking

Like crystal breaking at a note precisely pitched
sleep shatters. I lurch to the cry,
threading the night with soft
wheeshts of comfort.

She pulls at the breast, milk-tingled, stemming the weep and flow.
I gaze at the lash-stroked cheek, the down
of hair, as she empties the night
of wind-whirl,

owl shriek.
Cocooned in the gentled cage,
we do not feel the ice on the glass
or the wolf-winds breathing the curtains to a fierce frenzy.

Tony Curtis

Born in 1946 in Carmarthen and educated at universities in the U.K. and U.S.A., Tony Curtis is Professor of Poetry at the University of Glamorgan. He is the author of seven collections of poetry, the most recent being *War Voices,* and the editor of several books including *Wales: The Imagined Nation* and *The Art of Seamus Heaney.*

Taken for Pearls

In muddied waters the eyes of fishes
are taken for pearls.

As those two trout, little bigger than my hand then,
taken by spinner at Cresselly on an early

summer's day in the quiet afternoon
before the season's traffic. Only

a tractor in an unseen field
stitching the air like a canopy over it all.

And the taste of them pan-fried nose to tail
by my mother. The sweet flesh prised from

cages of the most skilfully carved bone.
I closed my eyes and she smiled for me.

The Death of Richard Beattie-Seaman
in the Belgian Grand Prix, 1939

Trapped in the wreckage by his broken arm
he watched the flames flower from the front end.
So much pain — *Holy Jesus, let them get to me* —
so much pain he heard his screams like music
when he closed his eyes — the school organ at Rugby
Matins with light slanting down
hot and heady from the summer's high windows.
Pain — his trousers welded by flame to his legs.
His left hand tore off the clouded goggles —
rain falling like light into the heavy trees,
the track polished like a blade.
They would get to him, they were all coming
all running across the grass, he knew.

The fumes of a tuned Mercedes smelt like
boot polish and tear gas — coughing, his screams rising
high out of the cockpit — high
away back to '38 Di Nurburgring.
He flew in with Clara
banking and turning the Wessex through a slow circle
over the scene — sunlight flashing off the line of cars,
people waving, hoardings and loudspeakers, swastikas
and the flags of nations lifted in the wind he stirred.
She held his arm tightly, her eyes were closed.
He felt strong like the stretched wing of a bird,
the course mapped out below him.
That day Lang and Von Brauchitsch and Caracciola
all dropped out and he did it — won
in the fourth Mercedes before a crowd of half a million
— the champagne cup, the wreath around his neck,
An Englishman the toast of Germany
The camera caught him giving a Hitlergruss.
Waving arms, shouts and faces, a mosaic
laid up to this moment — La Source — tight — the hairpin
in the trees — tight — La Source — keeping up the pace
Belgium — La Source hairpin too tight.

With the fire dying, the pain dying,
the voices blurred beneath the cool licks of rain.
To be laid under the cool sheets of rain.
A quiet with, just perceptible, engines roaring
as at the start of a great race.

My Father

My father is a shadow
growing from my feet.

This shadow grows from one minute
past the noon of my life
and trails me like water.

My father is mending all fifty-three of his cars.
He works in a garden shed
by the caged light of an inspection lamp.
The red glow at his lips shows constantly
small and fierce like an airliner overhead
or the startled eye of a fox.

Ash falls onto the greased parts
of the dynamo.
He hawks and spits through the door.

His hands and nails black with grease
come out from the old paint tin
he has filled with petrol.
Like rare birds they rise
their plumage glistening and sharp
spilling green and blue and silver.

Those hands that my forehead meets
briefly and shivering.
Those rough hands I run from
like the borders of a strange country.

Making Bread for *Sunblest*

To be with you
all that summer vacation
I made bread for *Sunblest* in north Wales.
Not so much a bakery, more a bread factory
with conveyor-belt proving of the machined dough,
conveyor-belt ovens where we stood all night
in the river of loaves, catching
the burning tins in our mittens
with awkward puppet-grasps and banging
the crisp ochre bricks out
on to the cooling racks. A crew
of students mucking in with the old hands,
men who'd been, in their time, real bakers,
moving now like automatons through the early hours.

And in the meal-breaks I'd strip
my white overalls to run the mile
to your house, scratch at your father's back-door:
a cup of tea from your mother, served discreetly,
away in the kitchen while the old man
glowered at his blaring TV
You'd walk me back to the gate, chilled in the air
and still flour-dusty for the jog back under
the stars. We'd kiss.
Across twenty years these things
return, distracting me tonight
as I rise, proving constant
in your practised hands.

Swimming Class

Our children are learning to save themselves.
From the pool, his shouts, their splashing and cries:
frog-legs, dog-paddle, flop-dives —
they ride the water, held by our breath.
We've wrapped their modest cocks with towels,

tousled and talced them dry, cowled like monks.
We pull the wet valves and the stale air farts out:
the floaters squash like rotten fruit.

When we have gone the instructor's smoke hangs
over the tiles. He watches his butt sizzle
in a stream of piss, wipes off the mirror's dew
and inflates his biceps and chest. Every week we push
them further to a length. The world beyond
is made by accidents. We love them and they could drown.

Ivy

The choking ivy we lopped and sawed and tore
and one day — yes, in a blast of anger — burned
from the old pear still clings.

As we axed and ripped the tentacles
it slacked its biceps, unclenched its fist.
I climbed and hacked while you
dragged great clumps of ivy to your bonfire.

But high in the thirty-foot summits
clogging this season's hard, sour pears
the last clutch of parched, rootless stuff
worn like a wig still weighs on the tree.

By October winds should have scattered the dead leaves
and you'll watch me climb again to snap
the final twists of brittle tendril.

At full stretch I shall prise them loose
then feed them down through the bare branches.
And you, my boy, will look up to me with impatience
like a climber at the bottom waiting for ropes.

Breaking Surface

Out of the oiled water
weeks later, they hoisted you, lovers
married in the cold depths of the docks.
And until the dredger's knock
and buckle against your car's roof,
they'd fictioned your runaway.
A sinful flight, snatched love in rented rooms,
incognito, with the scant luggage of a shame
friends and family presumed,
the strange newnesses they'd envied.
The loved, abandoned children calling your name.

Questions rise,
bubble and break the surface:
how was the bond made?
And where? Why
into the docks, such
grim and botched waters?
And what words, sucked
from the last air
before the rush of dark?
Such probings, metallic and cold.
Cold the kiss, the deepening cries.

Our comings and goings, trade
on the slop of water, wash over,
tread down such detritus as you.
The Sunday boys cast their bait
across the length of afternoon.
The weights find bottom and anchor.
Their lines crease the slick.

Nothing pulls.
No sound but the slapping sound
of stale trapped water.
Maybe drowned is best left drowned.

Coracle

Sea Oracle —
wattled water rider, sewin slayer,
Towy tossed when the tide rises.
Man-shell — two tortoises
crawling from the falling sun,
or the wings of a black moth.
Two halves of a cockleshell
drifting back to a whole.

One arm twisting like ivy
round the smooth paddle
to stir the water like thick cawl,
the other weighing the net's haul
from its slow semi-circle of river-trawl.
And then the unstrapped truncheon,
brought down for the sharp crack of bone,
the last slap of dispatch.

Thimbles worn against
the current's sharpening point
with their slung-between fish-pen,
gill-snagging, fin-trapping,
cow hair spun into strings
that play the deep song of the river.
The catch of silver
in the midas touch of moonlight.

Soup

One night our block leader set a competition:
two bowls of soup to the best teller of a tale.
That whole evening the hut filled with words —
tales from the old countries
of wolves and children
potions and love-sick herders
stupid woodsmen and crafty villagers,

73

Apple-blossom snowed from blue skies,
orphans discovered themselves royal.
Tales of greed and heroes and cunning survival,
soldiers of the Empires, the Church, the Reich.

And when they turned to me
I could not speak,
sunk in the horror of that place,
my throat a corridor of bones, my eyes
and nostrils clogged with self-pity.
'Speak,' they said, 'everyone has a story to tell.'
And so I closed my eyes and said:
'I have no hunger for your bowls of soup, you see
I have just risen from the Shabbat meal —
my father has filled our glasses with wine,
bread has been broken, the maid has served fish.
Grandfather has sung, tears in his eyes, the old songs.
My mother holds her glass by the stem, lifts
it to her mouth, the red glow reflecting on her throat,
I go to her side and she kisses me for bed.
My grandfather's kiss is rough and soft like an apricot.
The sheets on my bed are crisp and flat
like the leaves of a book...'.

I carried my prizes back to my bunk: one bowl
I hid, the other I stirred
and smelt a long time, so long
that it filled the cauldron of my head,
drowning a family of memories.

Portrait of the Painter Hans Theo Richter
and his wife Gisela in Dresden, 1933 — Otto Dix

This is the perfect moment of love —
Her arm around his neck,
Holding a rose.

Her wisps of yellow hair
The light turns gold.
Her face is the moon to his earth.

Otto's studio wall glows
With the warm wheat glow
Of the loving couple.

This is after the dark etchings,
The blown faces. This is after Bapaume —
The sickly greens, the fallen browns.

She is a tree, her neck a swan's curved to him.
His hands enclose her left hand
Like folded wings.

This is before the fire-storm,
Before the black wind,
The city turned to broken teeth.

It is she who holds the rose to him,
Theo's eyes which lower in contentment
To the surgeon's smock he wears for painting.

This is the perfect moment,
The painted moment
She will not survive.

This is before the hair that flames,
The face that chars. This is before
Her long arms blacken like winter boughs.

This is the harvest of their love,
It is summer in the soul,
The moment they have made together.

From Otto's window the sounds of the day —
The baker's boy calling, a neighbour's wireless
playing marches and then a speech.

Incident on a Hospital Train
from Calcutta, 1944

At a water-stop three hours out
the dry wail of brakes ground us down
from constant jolting pain to an oven
heat that filled with moans and shouts
from wards the length of six carriages.

We had pulled slowly up towards the summer
hills for coolness. They were hours distant,
hazy and vague. I opened the grimy
window to a rush of heat
and, wrapped in sacking, a baby

held up like some cooked offering from its mother —
Memsahib... meri buchee ko bachalo... Memsahib take —
pushed like an unlooked-for gift into my arms.
She turned into the smoke and steam.
I never saw her face.

As we lumbered off I unwrapped
a dirty, days-old girl, too weak for cries.
Her bird weight and fever-filled eyes
already put her out of our reach. By Murree Junction
that child would have emptied half our beds.

At the next water-stop my nurses left her.
The corporal whose arms had gone looked up at me
and said, 'There was nothing else to do'.
Gangrenous, he died at Murree a week later.
His eyes, I remember, were clear, deep and blue.

John Davies

Born in Port Talbot in 1944, John Davies has taught in the U.K. and the U.S.A. and currently lives in Prestatyn, north Wales. He is the author of three Seren collections, the most recent being *Flight Patterns*. He is also the editor of a textbook for using Anglo-Welsh poetry in schools, *The Streets and the Stars*. His new book of poetry, *Dirt Roads*, will appear in 1997.

In Port Talbot

By now it's like returning to a foreign town, especially
at night when the steelworks' odd familiar fever
flushes again faint red on walls and ceilings.
Its reverberations, too, this time I cannot hear
as silence. When cars stop smashing rain to spray
or after a train has dragged its chains across stone floors,
what remains is this, work's dying murmur.

Lying flat, the whole town breathes through stacks;
gouts of asthmatic coughing churn the sky.
All night in burnt air, an enormous radio
aglow with coiled circuits, aerials straining high,
blasts out selections from Smoke at ranked streets
with floatings of thick chords that echo for miles.
They drown, almost, the groundswell hum nearby.

Homes of the well-off on Pentyla have the best view
of the steelworks. The main road follows it obediently.
Running coastwards greased by rain, streets skidded
to this edge, finding metal had replaced the sea

with slabs that rear white-ridged with steam then stop.
All night, rolling in over the beached town
are breakers never seen, a thrumming like memory.

Look out on winter's thin streets. See how steel
lights up the whole town still. Although it shivers now
in November dreaming of steel's breaking point, its people —
kept from clean air but not each other — could tell how
common purpose, gathering, runs strongest
on hardest ground. As here where the land turned
overnight to metal, where smoke blooms in the window.

And when at last shared work's vibrations cease,
sharing itself will fade (as in the mining villages nearby)
with Keir Hardie's dream, with Bethanias long since ghosts,
down history's shaft. Difference and indifference will untie
taut bonds of work that cramp yet forged here a community;
then old South Wales will have to start a New. Meanwhile
reverberations still, slow leavings, long goodbye.

How to Write Anglo-Welsh Poetry

It's not too late, I suppose....
You could sound a Last Post or two,
and if you can get away with saying
what's been said, then do.

First, apologise for not being able
to speak Welsh. Go on: apologise.
Being Anglo-anything is really tough;
any gaps you can fill with sighs.

And get some roots, juggle names like
Taliesin and ap Gwilym, weave
a Cymric web. It doesn't matter what
they wrote. Look, let's not be naïve.

Now you can go on about the past
being more real than the present —
you've read your early R.S. Thomas,
you know where Welsh Wales went.

Spray place-names around. Caernarfon.
Cwmtwrch. Have, perhaps, a Swansea
sun marooned in Glamorgan's troubled
skies; even the weather's Welsh, see.

But a mining town is best, of course,
for impact, and you'll know what to say
about Valley Characters, the heart's dust
and the rest. Read it all up anyway.

A quick reference to cynghanedd
always goes down well; girls are cariad;
myth is in; exile, defeat, hills...
almost anything Welsh and sad.

Style now. Nothing fancy: write
all your messages as prose then chop
them up — it's how deeply red and green
they bleed that counts. Right, stop.

That's it, you've finished for now —
just brush your poems down: dead, fluffed
things but your own almost. Get
them mounted in magazines. Or stuffed.

Barry John

who tacked like a yacht
through breakers,
tidewreck where he'd

been, whose arms, hips,
swapped fly half-
truths tacklers grasped

too late, was a spool
casually unwound
around sharp eyes

lining him up just right.
Then he'd crossed
their lines, parachuted

in, pass master
of the national art,
straightforward veering.

Border Incident

Its churchy reverence for food, those waiters grave
amongst candles, made the place seem empty.
My waiter (André apparently) had passed
the collection plate while I sipped coffee, lingering.
To tip or not? The service had been quiet, fast;
short of loose change, I could always give a blessing.

They were being shown to the table next to mine
as I glanced up. Fiftyish, officer material, good school —
she was in charge, I thought. His was a bald front
of managerial class, a pink all-seeing lens,
as he rearranged his hands before him then sat blunt
at his polished desk, its line of silver pens.

André approached. 'Good evening, madam'. She bowed
as he passed the menu. 'Good evening, s—'.
He peered down, served him an eager stare.
'It's *you*, Mr. Prys-Evans! How are you then?
How are things in Bont?' And he pulled up a chair.
Bald Prys-Evans froze, seemed to count a long slow ten

but 'Fine, Jack, fine,' replied at last. They chatted
awhile — Jack had left South Wales in '75, I learned —
while the wife's crisp skirt breathed rustling sighs.

As they ordered food, Jack scribbling in biro
on his open palm, I saw her close her eyes.
Three different kinds of wonder watched him go.

The main course came and went and I sat there
riveted. I'd learnt quite a lot about Bont by then,
about bank manager Prys-Evans too, whose steely
wife seemed about to close their joint account for good.
Nodding, he'd suffered all Jack's homesick bonhomie
as if about to explode, knowing he never would.

When they'd gone, as I was leaving at last,
'Nice to see folks from home,' I said to Jack.
'Aye, Prys-Evans rules the roost there.' He smiled.
'But I fixed his meal all right. See his face
all the time he was eating — drove him wild,
I did! Bont, I can't stand the bloody place'.

Howard

In town, a long sad face shunting a rumble
turned into Howard Roberts from Philadelphia
tracking his roots. I owe America.
Tour buses roared, sawing Wales in half
as we talked, and, keen, I showed him our pet castle.
Ghost yawns closing one eye then his other
suggested that belonging might come pricey.

West in thrashed acres where he found
most valleys are depressions between faults,
farms and quarries mourned by sheds
proved rain's not always kind to withered roots.

The bar foamed. Stan folded in laughter, an ancient
head juggling false teeth, a Punch and Judy show.
Howard wasn't unimpressed but shunned groups of more
than one — eyes sad about their wicked weight
of brow turned down his mouth, the grin a wince.

81

His voice trailing off in search of entrances
or exits said it wasn't a past he needed.

He stayed long enough anyway to lose his tan,
sing with the choir once and leave antique shops
looted. Whole bunches of choice bric
and brac were bedded lovingly for transplant
so though he found not a single root
quite a lot of the old country went with him, you bet.

Five Canoes

The sky has tilted west, spilling
a river before us, canoeing us asway
where flatness splashed by new scatterings
breaks and the glitter covers our trails
washed under feathery brimmings-over
of trees whose swell the banks ride out.
Together, we've been chosen by this surge
nothing can steer us from and even
if we wanted to there is no going back.

It's out in midstream we find our level,
midstream again. The current straddled,
now we ride at ease. Those edges though, ripped
white asizzle with risk, with promises,
broad habit guides us from — not the sliding
glacial water. We stay with what we know,
which is not ourselves hunched inside
objects we possess on another open road.
Drifting, we slip apart content.

Sun shines us on. All that I see once more
is how I look at things, there's no
submersion in waters of the middle way.
Still, what heaves against our paddles
also drives us on. And at Rockport Bridge

in shallows so clear and flat
only the pebbles' shine says Water,
I'm in glitter again, just arrivals and
departures count, the rest a means of progress.

Things to do when the town's closed

Our choir dressed as guerrilla butlers
has driven the holidaymakers back.
It is September. Seagulls
are critics prying over spilt ink.
The town's scraped off its silver lining
to get at the cloud instead.

In search of a bit of life,
Ron has started taxidermy, juggling
bags of skin like a homicidal vet.
They grin from furry cells,
near-squirrels.
You can't keep a good man up.

And Mr. S has emptied his firm's safe.
Self-bloodied, he faked
assault then described the villain
so well for the police photofit,
like a shout his own face rang out.

On the library wall: ANACKY.
Draughts from the Mersey Tunnel quicken
across the Dee. Wait,
slow down
at the station.
You can find yourself elsewhere.

Balloons were released in August
from Ffrith Beach for Holiday Fun
with addressed labels. W's returned
all the way from Builth. His prize?

First cash, soon a court appearance:
winds blew north that day so how come W's balloon
went south? Well, live in town
and wind is just a ghost. The label went
via his aunt in Builth, both ways by post.

Yesterday, high on a ladder with acres
to paint, Mr. S was whistling 'Born Free'.
And although the Pleasant Sunday Afternoon Society
now meets all week, although the slipper women
at the launderette seem lively
and waves roll up in fits watching dunes
fail to outwit caravans,
it's a bad time.

We are alone together.
Even our jeweller's stopped twinkling.
You can't help but feel
someone out there might be planning chainsaw
psychiatry or florist pressing.

Bards

*At the Caerwys eisteddfod of 1568, a permit system
sought to distinguish genuine poets from the rest.
Licence applicants were judged by experts.*

Northward they flew, flushed warblers,
waves of wordsmiths in a whir
much vaunted, pally valour
plumed in a valley pallor.
Some were skylarks, some thickskinned
parrots on a palsied wind.

Starred high fliers, hawks of sense,
were launched on poetic licence
but most raved at rejection's slip,
with tumbled owls found kinship.
Showbirds in dylanesquish fits

rewarmed scrambled eggs of wit;
doves of peace with sharp beaks,
hair-breasted, brandished leeks.
Bards sat slurring whole sestets
of bitter and sounding wet,
freethinkers with three thoughts —
then they dived south distraught
under poetry's bright shield:
egoes rampant on a brazen field.

Stern Caerwys, true arts council,
steel in the memory still.
You cleared from the land its host
of cuckoos for ever almost,
and two large truths you left us.
It's a long haul to Parnassus.
Most of us winged by words
are essentially home birds.

Jean Earle

Jean Earle was born in Bristol in 1909 but brought up in the Rhondda valley. She lived in various parts of Wales for most of her life and only began to publish her work in the late 1970s. Her most recent collection is *The Sun in the West* which followed the 1990 publication of her well-received *Selected Poems*. She currently lives in Shrewsbury with her family.

Jugged Hare

She mourned the long-ears
Hung in the pantry, his shot fur
Softly dishevelled. She smoothed that,
Before gutting — yet she would rather
Sicken herself, than cheat my father
Of his jugged hare.

A tender lady, freakish as the creature —
But resolute. She peeled it to its tail.
Oh, fortitude! Her rings sparked in and out
Of newspaper wipes. Blood in a bowl,
Sacrificial gravy. A rarely afforded
Bottle of port.

She sustained marriage
On high events, as a child plays house.
Dramas, conciliations —
Today, the hare. She sent me out
To bury the skin,
Tossed the heart to the cat.

She was in full spate.

Fragrance of wine and herbs
Blessed our kitchen, like the hare's dessert
Of wild thyme; or like his thighs
As though braised by God. She smiled
And dished up on willow,
Having a nice touch in framing
One-off scenarios.

After the feast, my father was a lover
Deeply enhanced.
I heard them go to bed.
Kissing — still inside her picture.
Later, I heard her sob
And guessed it was the hare
Troubled her. My father slept,
Stunned with tribute. She lay now
Outside her frame, in the hare's dark

Hating her marital skills
And her lady-hands, that could flense a hare
Because she wooed a man.
In years to come,
I understood.

In the Night

When we were children, out to tea,
The child of the house showed us his toys,
Their glancing novelties
And fit loveliness to do as he said.

He was beautiful too; elegant as a bird
Up trees and over walls. He had acquired techniques
Far beyond our stodge of childishness.

We riffled his books; bright pictures, cruel stories,
Taxed our understanding. Then, he was sarcastic.

He stood in a puddle and stamped.
Dirt — and rainbows —
Flew all over our clean dresses.

He invited us to the top of the house
And shut us in the dark attic.

Such an entertainer! Yet, never once
Did he look straight at us — merely put on his tricks,
Miracles of display. Considering, in particular,
The attic — I have wondered, sometimes,
Whether God is not like that boy?

But He tells me, He is not. In the night He tells me,
When it is often imperative to know.
A felled tree once assured me
He is to be trusted —
And a film where the crocodile carried her eggs
In her jaws, so tenderly, without hurting any
Against the craters of her terrible snap.

It must be fault in myself, how seldom
Anything human convinces me
God is not like that boy....

Honesty

Always a 'snapper-up of trifles' —
Jars from a skip, those rubber bands
Postmen let fly —
Some sad kitten —
After her trip, she brought me such a thing,
A seed of honesty
From Wordsworth's garden.

Had she any idea
How it pleased me? Only as tourist
At Dove Cottage had she ever heard
Of William and Dorothy

Who may well have trodden the soil
This seed sprang from....

Sowing the scarlet beans; or when Dorothy
Set herbs by moonlight. When she worked alone,
Grieving for William — who had taken joy
Of their life together into his stern hold
And gone for Mary.

Intense and ardent hearts! The seed sent up
A thin stalk, has managed a few flowers
Of a sharp magenta. She who stole me this
Finds it not worth the snatch,
Having no clue
How eloquent to me — yes, as a friend's dress
Seen against time and light,
Its colour is.

Afterwards

The surviving half of the earth
Shuddered: centred the sun:
Went on turning.

With that year's decline
The migrant birds
Followed their stars
To alternate summer
And the steadied trades
Carried such butterflies and moths
As make these odysseys — mindless
Whether they journeyed as birds or insects.

For some were effortless travellers,
Catching a lift, duveted against windwarps
By stronger flyers. Within each skull —
Insect or bird —

Delicate, fierce magnets
Locked on the goal, moving in cloud
Or vee formations,
To the summer land.

Likewise, through immemorial
By-ways of seas, fishes and eels
urgently pressed towards the birth-rivers.

And there was nothing....

Nesting materials
Nor caterpillars, nor the inherited dance
Of ephemera, nor the expected
Certain alighting places.
The home waters ran no taste
Of arrival. Manifestations of death
Clogged in the bays. By natural law,
No U-turn possible....

They hovered awhile —
Sensing some predatory cull
More ruthless than usual —
Till the overstretched wings
Weakened and fell. The insect pheromones
Received no messages. On the bad tides
New phosphorescence
Dulled — and stank.

That was the season when there were — for once —
No human predators.

Static

Stripping off her clothes, in the dark,
Their stuffs flashed out a gentle lightning
About her legs; and being off,
Lay dead.

She thought,
'Is it the essence of myself,
Practising that stroke
When it leaves the head —
Taking the heartbeat with it —
And joins thunder,
Rolling a luminous birth
Out of life's dress?
That will slip — so —
Cling — so —
Flash. And, being off,
Lie dead...?'

Stillborn

There was a child born dead.

Time has bleached out the shocking insult,
Ageing has cicatrised the body's wound.

Still I do not like to prune bushes
That push to the sun...
Nor put my brush into the spider's house
Where she keeps her children,
Darting with terrible life.

With reluctance, I gouge potatoes
Sprouting intently in a dark bag.

Furtive, I slip one into the earth.
'Grow!' I say. 'Grow, if you must....'

Wife and Dolphin

Sunrise gulls, each one glittered
On a raft of diamonds. The loosed rope
Shimmering....

And out between Cradle and Cat
To bait the pots. Brooding there,
Alone in the boat.

A hot-tempered man.

Sometimes, he saw his wife's face
On the water glare. He had struck her a blow
And she had left. Would never return —
That was her nature.

Lip tide —
With a light haze, lifting —
Was her eyes' very colour. The gathered sea
Loomed, whitened, parted on Cradle and Cat,
Foundering over.

He would chat up the dolphin
That was pleasant with him.
Had it play stick
Like a dog, watched it take fish,
Flash, swallow — jokingly neat. He dived once
Under the silver flump of it,
Touched his hand to belly and flick,
Smiling snout.

It became his own —
But free, he wanted that —
Looking for him to sight and amuse it.
He, too, was entertained,
In morose depths delighted.

Saving for a new boat,
He would take summer people out
To see the dolphin. Two went with him —
Showman types —
He soon guessed they had plans for it.

What to do? Temper made trouble.
When he was sure of their intent,
He would go alone
Where the full greenswing
Sets away from Cradle and Cat,
Far out...

And play stick with the dolphin —
Hit it on the nose,
Hard. It would never come back.

That is its nature.

Your Aura

Somebody said she saw your aura
From across the room. Not disbelief
But jealousy, brought me out in a heat.
'What colour?'
'Blue....'

Loving you so, why can't I see
This embellishment? It well may be
that you wear such a scary frill
Around your head. Gentle and shy,
You are a far better candidate
For an aura than I — yet, in a crowd,
Briefly removed from me,
and a stranger spotting your aura,
I felt low.

If anyone has the gift
For seeing auras, it should be me....
Being one to notice
What most people don't. The risen sun
Firing my plants, pointing the hairs
With diamond (that is how it might be,
Your aura?). Or I glance aside
From love, to note a blanket-hem

Shimmering double, looked at close
To the moony eye: or how a switched-off lamp
Blots on the sudden dark
Blooms of its shape....

If she did see your aura,
I have a right to it, too.
'What colour?'
'Blue....'

Gran and Gramp at the Fireworks

Briskly, they spooned us out of their car
Along night pavements. Trees
Cumbered the walking-space with roots, so like
The tall grandchildren, high with windy leaves
And authority.
We achieved a bank
Above dark water. Here, they set us chairs
Which they had carried, swung from the hip
Lightly as keys. Docile, we perched,
Wise to (but not voicing) rising damp.

Then the shooting began, breaking above the town
Jewelled umbrellas. A band came to us,
Not too loud. The nervous river
Reddened and blued. Such magical storms
Burst overhead. Perhaps our last?

Certainly, not so many more
Gropings into the wild, dangerous night....

They did not say much
But stood behind our mild exclamations
As two flares
Might wait, primed to explode at a touch
Into coloured fire. Ourselves,
As we were once....

Christine Evans

Born in 1943 in Yorkshire, Christine Evans came to her father's
birthplace in Pwllheli to teach English in 1967. She still lives and
works in Llŷn and is the author of four Seren collections, the most
recent being *The Island of Dark Horses* (1995), a celebration of
Bardsey Island, a site of medieval pilgrimage in northwest Wales.

Callers

It is always a shock when they take off their caps,
Those neighbouring farmers who call at our house.
They have to, of course, to have something to roll
Or to press or to twist in their blunt, nervous hands;
But it makes them instantly vulnerable
With their soft bald spots or thinning forelocks.
They seem at once smaller, and much more vivid:
Leaping out of type to personality.

The smell of their beasts comes in with them,
Faint as the breath of growing things in summer,
Rich, as the days draw in, with cake and hay and dung.
They are ill at ease in the house:
One feels they would like to stamp and snort,
Looking sideways, but have been trained out of it —
As with leaving mucky boots beside the door.

Only small, swarthy men with the friendly smell on them;
Yet walls press close and the room seems cluttered.
I am glad to go and make obligatory tea
As their voices sway, slow with the seasons,
And, ponderously, come to the point.

Summer in the Village

Now, you can see
where the widows live:
nettles grow tall and thistles seed
round old machinery.
Hayfields smooth under the scythe
simmer with tussocks;
the hedges begin to go,
and the bracken floods in.

Where the young folk have stayed on
gaudy crops of caravans
and tents erupt in the roadside fields;
Shell Gifts, Crab Sandwiches, To Let,
the signs solicit by the gates, left open
where the milk churns used to stand;
and the cash trickles in.

'For Sale' goes up again
on farms the townies bought with good intentions
and a copy of *The Whole Earth Guide;*
Samantha, Dominic and Willow play
among the geese and goats while parents in the pub
complain about Welsh education and the dole.
And a new asperity creeps in.

Now, you will see
the tidy management of second homes:
slightly startled, old skin stretched,
the cottages are made convenient.
There are boats with seats;
dogs with the work bred out of them
sit listlessly by garden chairs on Kodakcolor lawns;
and all that was community seeps out.

First Lamb

Limp and sodden as old rags, stained
Like rust with the delay, it's eased round
And unfolded out of all her warmth;
Airseal at nose and mouth
Ripped clear, and shaken
Into breathing. Now the ewe must lick him....
But she will only stare in horror
As the struggling flesh that,
Meshed in mucus, seems persistent
To be part of her again.

She has never been caught before, this one.
How she ran, preferring talons in her belly
To the unknown grip of hands.
She wheels and stamps
Though nothing but the north wind pens her —
And this stranded creature, mouth already
Seeking in the angle of determination
Like a daffodil's blind aiming at the sky.

The afterbirth, a pendulum of blood,
Swinging, startles her into stampede:
Each step back's a slow defeat

And when suddenly he pushes out
A trickling cry — thin as a bird out to sea —
Inexorably, she is wound in.
By nightfall, she has the hunch
Of habitual solicitude; he,
A living lustre, glimmering
Like rare moss against her steadiness
In a dry, committed sleep.
Her eyes are unflinching in the torchlight.
Her neck is stretched, her nostrils full of him,
And she has even found a new voice.

She has only to listen
To learn tenderness, to be right.

Exchange

I am doing *The Red Pony*
With 3B. Despite their appetite
For murder, horror films
And modern cannibals, they
Are easily moved
By animals. Aloud, they wonder
About the first that shared our lives:
Dogs, they agree, and orphaned goats,
Suggests the girl whose mother keeps
The wholefood shop. But 'Cows, Miss?'
They do not see have anything,
Save meat and milk, to give.
So I do not try to tell them

How with the first cow that we bought,
Old, scarred and belly-sagged
With breeding, for a time I found
An old affinity, a new
Exchange. She had rosettes like flowers
Hidden in her glossy hide;
Her throat was soft as catkins
In the sun. She stood
Hock-deep in meadowsweet
Sighing as I milked her;
On winter mornings, breathed its fragrance
Through the stone cowshed. I warmed my hands
On her blackness, my heart
With her trust.

It was February, before dawn, hard frost
Squeezing the land to silence
When we loaded her. The concrete
Glistened like black slate.
It took my voice,
My hand on her flank, to get her
Stumbling up the ramp.
'Well done, Missus!' And I stood back

Smiling, as the bolts went home.
Eighty pence per kilo
On the hook. She was barren,
Useless. But I am glad
It was too dark to see her eyes.

Knife

I have a kitchen knife so sharp
It is a scalpel in my hand.
I watch the shadow of the blade
Slide underneath the surface, slicing through
Creamy intricate unseen connections.
Drawing it across a lump of unscored pork
I seem to hear the stuck pig shriek
Its hair salt-white and bristling still
Against hand spread to hold it down.

Earlier I made delicate incisions
Into the eye of a grapefruit
And a long slit in a trapped hare's belly
To lift its still-warm workings out —
A dark blood-spongy fungus.
Vegetables yield fewer mysteries:
Sprouts I rip are small cold stones
But I carry a cauliflower in from the plot
Snugged like a head against my breast

Dew starting from it, big tears of surprise.
Once I worked all day cutting
In a field of winter caulis, methodically
Moving up and down the rows until the cool clean
Smell of slashed leaves grew rank about us
And women stooping to each blank white face
Felt like a ritual or a battlefield.
Our arms were aching but a complicity
Of hand and eye
And the rhythm of the knife
Swept us through, past sunset.

Lucy's Bones

Most of our bodies will melt
letting all they ever were leak out.
Between the fires and the fresh ruins
folds of white fat
hiss and gutter till flesh flows;
but her bones will arch in the earth
not gently flexed as if in sleep
but sound as boat-staves, seasoned
timber that takes two generations to give way.

Mole-mouthed as a lover
rot will move over her
a charge of blue seed
quivering her thighs, flooding
the bright, packed silks, the slit reefs
prying under fingernails
disentangling white stalks
for the petals to fall free
and alchemise to a stencil.

Then her long bones will be
galleries of sighing
her ribcage a cathedral.
The wings of her shoulders
go on promising horizons, her pelvis
pause at the edge of its double question
the little carpal and the tarsal bones
lie orderly, arranged like pieces
waiting to clatter into prophecy.

The shell of her skull shall brim with honey:
in each eye-cave a chrysalis
stir toward the shrouded sun.
Ladybird and velvet mite and leaf beetle
seedpearls of snails' eggs
nest in the sockets of her knuckles.
In each dry crack, a patient germ:
primrose and birch and rosemary,
white roots of fern to weave a launchpad.

She should be lodged in topmost branches
stirred at the heart of her own green storm
but her smile will shine out
through blinded ground, through deafened wind
because she stayed eager all her life
kept her face to the edge
constantly spending
and was charged with such brightness
waste cannot claim her.

Morning Watch

Inside, the lighthouse is gloss-painted
Like prison or a hospital. Too hot.
The radio stammers, blurts, then hums.
Sport or men with guns mutter on a screen
All look at, no-one watches, in an acrid haze
Of Players' Number 6 or roll-your-owns.
Nestlé's Milk coffee, or floating Marvel,
Is the only indication you're offshore
(Formica buckling, tin teapot, pedal bin)
Till you catch reflections of the symmetry
Of a nursery tale — for there are three
Of everything — three chairs with thin foam
Cushions that slide down as soon
As sat on, three tea-towels, bookshelves;
Out in the garden, three lavatory cells
Three toolsheds, pigsties, garden plots gone wild.

And three pale unfocussed sedentary men
Sleeping, eating, being awake
On or off according to a roster.

Baz steps out, shirt-sleeved, to do the Met
(which numbers on the weather form he'll tick)
Acres of white foam, the air
A wide blue yawn he slams in from:
'Christ! It's cold enough out there —'
Their laughter drowns the thrum of engines.

But sometimes, he's confided, in the small hours
Sneking the white gate close behind him
He truants, leaving light in its tower cage
Where homing seabirds grunt and scream and fall
To tread salt turf springy with old roots
And stand like a captain in the wind
Reading the dark stretch of his deck
Sensing the night miles crossed
Till his heartbeat's only a flicker
His cigarette a brave red throb
On the seabed of the floating stars.

His daylight brain thinks it forgotten
But in off-duty dreams, a hundred miles
From sea, he feels the island dip and steady;
Glimpses the black walls building, pushed astern
Tumbling, crawling, gathering, re-gathering
Outrun, but following.

Case History

There was a boy of twelve who'd never learned
To speak. Farm-bred, he had not understood
That he was more than livestock — turned
To dogs for company, came running for his food
With cats or chickens and woke with no surprise
At owls' homecoming or stars' breath on his face.
I saw him when they brought him in. His eyes
Were clear as sunlit water, held a space
We promptly crammed with language. Beyond reach
Soft wordless songs, the colours in wet-stone
He loved; grass-smell; the old humanity of touch.
His brightness died, and we began to realise
Speech wakes in us so confident, so soon
What deeper dumbnesses might it disguise?

On Retreat

She has been, she tells me, so careful
Of her children — cautious even of care,
But keeping them free from cold
And flies and hunger, responsible
About check-ups at the dentist
And quiet hours for homework.
Always, she would keep from them
The bare boards and the shouting
Of her childhood

Rejoicing that they have inherited
so little to reproach her for, no sign
Of short sight, crooked toes or asthma.
The easy gladness of their growing
Kept the cold wind from her back.
But now the girl
Weeps until her gaze is empty
As a wave in winter, starves her body
Because humanity, she screams, is rotten

And the small son
Whose earth-brown eyes were warm
With mischief or with wondering
Begins to ask why there's no cure
For cruelty. Now she must explain

The fairness that she's taught them
Is a game; not all the monsters
Can be spelled away in talking,
And being happy
Is a visitation or an accident.
She's here to work out how
To find some focus for the fear —
That the painless childhood she has shared with them
Has not cost the toughness to survive.

Peter Finch

Peter Finch was born in 1947 in Cardiff where he still lives. He is the manager of the HMSO Oriel Bookshop in Cardiff and an expert on poetry and small presses. A noted and prolific critic, performer, author and editor, he has also learned Welsh. His *Selected Poems* appeared in 1987. His new book, *Useful,* will arrive in 1997.

A Welsh Wordscape

1.

To live in Wales,

Is to be mumbled at
by re-incarnations of Dylan Thomas
in numerous diverse disguises.

Is to be mown down
by the same words
at least six times a week.

Is to be bored
by Welsh visionaries
with wild hair and grey suits.

Is to be told
of the incredible agony
of an exile
that can be at most
a day's travel away.

And the sheep, the sheep,
the bloody flea-bitten Welsh sheep,
chased over the same hills
by a thousand poetic phrases
all saying the same things.

To live in Wales
is to love sheep
and to be afraid
of dragons.

2.

A history is being re-lived,
a lost heritage
is being wept after
with sad eyes and dry tears.

A heritage
that spoke beauty to the world
through dirty fingernails
and endless alcoholic mists.

A heritage
that screamed that once,
that exploded that one holy time
and connected Wales
with the whirlpool
of the universe.

A heritage
that ceased communication
upon a death, and nonetheless
tried to go on living.

A heritage
that is taking
a long time to learn
that yesterday cannot be today

and that the world
is fast becoming bored
with language forever
in the same tone of voice.

Look at the Welsh landscape,
look closely,
new voices must rise,
for Wales cannot endlessly remain
chasing sheep into the twilight.

The Tattoo

At the ferro-concrete bike sheds
I pass a love-note to Veronica.
I wear long trousers and brylcream now
but her only interest is proven prowess.
I tattoo her name on my arm in Quink
with a penknife and show her.
She is unimpressed.
She goes out with a big ted from the fifth
who pisses over bog doors when you're in there.
He wears knuckle-dusters and can make a noise like a fart
with his armpit. Everyone is scared.
At break the Head tells me
that only criminals and soldiers sport tattoos
and sends me home to remove it.
My mother refuses. There is a dispute.
Magnificently my photograph
appears in the paper. Schoolboy Banned.
Our family are resolute.

It is over when by mistake
I wash a week later
and the whole thing goes.
I return to school a hero
where after assembly Veronica smiles
and the big ted breaks my nose.

Putting Kingsley Amis in the Microwave

I trowel the tear
in the flat roof felt
with black mastic.
Beneath on the bookshelves,
where the rain has reached
Kingsley Amis swells
like a row of fat Englishmen.

In the microwave
when I dry him
his heart turns dark
and his words unreadable.

It is what age does for you.

In time the roof will again fail
but that'll be fixable.

Winners

These people are always the ones in front.
They are taller than you they wear hats or have
huge high-rise hair-dos like Little Richard.
They are wide. Their shoulder pads are bad news.
They stretch out sideways blocking all avenues of sight.
You glimpse daylight through moving armpits
and in the gap between thighs. It's tough.
They step back into you talking
swelling enormously as they come.
What you thought was a wrist waving
becomes a backside of wallet pockets
turning through ninety without looking.
You ask for credentials but they'll
have been there anyway or owned one
or done it before or had their poems published in the *New Yorker*,
and even if you can get to grips with the

counter edge by having a long reach they
will have ways of drowning you.
Their voices will swell delivering jokes at full throttle
spraying spittle like lawn sprinklers
hands out, windmilling,
and the whole head of the queue contact
will be reduced to memory.
Everyone talking, scribbling, phoning,
putting in bids, flashing calculators, waving,
and you, gripping your fists white,
will wonder if you are invisible.
Pinch, punch,
and you are.
No other explanation.

Kipper on the Lips

O Cod,
I feel a right prawn.
Try to kipper outside the cinema.
Obviously the wrong plaice.
Welcoming bream turns into a foul mackerel,
next minnow she's slapping my face.
I'm amazed. What a dolphin to do.
Have I got halibutosis? A stickle back?
Squid in my trousers? No way.
I'm just a flash haddock after her turbots
Look at this conger eel I say.
But she's into big bivalves
and long-distance gurnards,
so I flounder.
What an elver time to distrust
your encrustation.
The sea trout's out, I'm a failure.
She goes off with a sperm whale.
I light up a bloater.

Ex-Smokes Man Writes Epic

eleven paragraphs on persuasion

1. Illusions

Breathe in. Place hot end in mouth. Close lips tightly. Blow.
Smoke pours out through filter.

Brown fingertips, nicotine traces.
This is the mark of a man.

Breath through handkerchief.
Look at the stain.

Cigarette in ear.

Double smoke rings through nostrils.

Move cigarette from nose
to mouth without using hands.

2. Exotica

Three cigarettes in mouth simultaneously.

Break wind. Light gas with glowing
stub held close to trousers.

3. Art

Blue Book, Passing Cloud, Gold Flake,
Three Tuns, Black Cat, Senior Service,
Cape to Cairo, Domino,
Ten pack, Van Gough, Tan mackintosh,
cool posture, hard type, pure hype.

4. Pain

Rip skin off lower lip with Woodbine.

Grip slips down shaft stuck to mouth by
lip blood. Burn fingertips.

Lighted end of cheap French fag falls out
and enters shoe.

Kingsize concertinerd into face by door slam.
Chest set alight by falling debris.

Benson and Hedges used for gesture in cinema
sets light to lacquered beehive of woman sitting in front of you.
Use of aerosol to subdue flame only makes matters worse.
Conflagration finally fire-hosed by manager wearing dinner suit.
Tell-tale dibbies found beneath your seat.
Thrown out for being under-age.

5. Vandalism

Brown stain on ceiling over bed.

Brown stain on walls in living-room.

Brown stain on toilet cistern.

Burn marks on dressing table.

Burn marks on kitchen shelf.

Burn marks on lid of record player.

Hole in carpet.

Singe marks on ties, shirts, lapels, sandwiches.

I once found a fag end in a meat pastie
and a bit of cork-tip in a tin of corned beef.

ha ha
ho ho.

6. Health

Cure? cough I don't cough care cough enough
can't be cough easy cough cough
cough cough can cough it
I ought cough to cough
shit cough cough stop cough
cough cough
cough.

7. Politics

but then again why should I?

8. Sociology

My grandfather lived to be 80.

9. Religion

If God hadn't wanted us to smoke
he wouldn't have given us lungs.

10. Sex

Panatella owner seeks ashtray.
No risk — built in filter.

11. Final Appeal

Ladies and Gentlemen,
consider the following:

a) T.S. Eliot smoked a pipe.
b) Cowboy Copas could roll a cheroot with one hand
while sitting on a horse.

Both are dead
or so I'm told.
I rest my case.

Severn Estuary ABC

A is a hat. Sun on my head.
B binoculars I'm using
C across the water. Largest concentration.
D is design. Planned
E in Europe. Believe that.
F is mud flats, wading birds
G for godwit, green sandpiper, grey plover
H is heavy population, heavy water.
I'm informed. I watch TV. My hat is
Just there to stop the sun burning.
Know what does it?
L is little suns in bottles. Heat.
M is the mighty atom.
N for no trouble in Oldbury, Hinkley Point, Berkeley.
Old stuff, I know. They're not sure.
P soup of a public explanation.
Quantity before quality. The fuel of the future.
R is rich someone's been salting somewhere. There's
                                              always someone.
Severn seeped solid. Sold down the river.
T is truth. Piece of fiction.
Ah yes.
U is understanding. It's safe.
V is very safe. Formation of ducks. Skinhead. Thatcher.
We buy it.
X marks the spot. The insidious ingress. The cancer.
Why don't we do something?
Z is the sound of us listening.

Catherine Fisher

Catherine Fisher was born in 1957 in Newport, Gwent where she still lives. A noted author of novels for young people, her second Seren volume of poetry, *The Unexplored Ocean (1995)*, features a sequence based on the eighteenth century journals of James Hartshill, a traveller on the voyages of Captain James Cook.

Immrama

First there was the island of the darkness.
When we rowed from there
the light was desolation for us.

And I remember a house with a golden chessboard
where we played too long.
What we lost I cannot remember.

As you go on it gets harder. Each landfall
an awakening of sorrows,
guile or treachery, the enticement of pleasures.

I lost my brother at the house of feathers,
good men at the harper's table.
There are always those who would hold us back.

You get used to the voices, the clinging fingers;
in every port the warning
'Beyond here is nothing but the sea'.

Islands of glass, islands of music and berries,
the isle of the locked door,
citadels and beaches where we dared not land,

these are behind us. Daily, the delirium rises;
it may be that smudge
on the horizon is a trick of my eyes.

And would we know that land if we should find it?
They say the scent of apples
wafts on the water; there is honey, hum of bees,

salmon leap into the boat. They say the others,
the lost ones, laugh on the sand.
But behind them, who are those strangers crowding the cliffs?

Snake-bite

Today is the day she will shed her skin;
she does not know it.
On fabric flowers butterflies alight;
long, cool-tongued grasses lick her heels,
tantalise basking
fingers, supine in sunlight.

This is the day the film will fall
from her eyes, as the wind passes,
rustling its insinuation
to the blind blue skies,
and zig-zag flickers of ochre
fleck the green uneasy grasses.

Soon she will cast it aside, the old,
split, papery wrapping;
through the red heat behind the eyelid, drift
and drone of wasps,
the subtlest beast of all the field
is bringing its bright gift.

And maybe today she will start again;
slough off old vagaries,
burst constriction, dull colour,
glisten, breathe, move with ease.
The grasses whisper. And look,
her eyes are open.

Severn Bore

Somewhere out there the sea has shrugged its shoulders.
Grey-green masses slip, rise, gather
to a ripple and a wave, purposeful, arrowing up
arteries of the land. Brown and sinuous, supple
as an otter, nosing upstream under the arching
bridge, past Chepstow, Lydney, Berkeley where a king
screamed; Westbury, where old men
click stopwatches with grins of satisfaction;
slopping into the wellingtons of watchers,
swamping the nests of coots, splashing binoculars.
And so to Minsterworth meadows where Ivor Gurney's ghost
walks in sunlight, unforgotten; past lost
lanes, cow-trodden banks, nudging the reeds,
lifting the lank waterweed,
flooding pills, backwaters, bobbing the floats
of fishermen, the undersides of leaves and boats,
and gliding, gliding over Cotswold's flawed
reflection, the sun swelling, the blue sky scored
with ripples, fish and dragonfly, stirred
by the drip and cloop of oars; and finally, unheard,
washing into the backstreets of town to lie
at the foot of the high
cathedral, prostrate, breathless,
pilgrim from a far place;
refugee
from the ominous petulance of the sea.

St. Tewdric's Well

Toad on the soft black tarmac knows it's there;
screened by deadnettle, tumbled with ivy.
He enters the water like a devotee,
anointed with bubbles.

If you lean over, your shadow shrouds him;
dimly your eyes find watersnails
down on the deep green masonry, and coins,
discarded haloes.

Tewdric's miracle, not even beautiful,
slowly effacing itself in exuberant nettles,
its only movement the slow clouds,
the sun's glinting ascension.

Lost in the swish of grasses, the hot road,
blown ladybirds, soft notes from a piano;
and over the houses the estuary grey as a mirror,
its islands stepping-stones for Bran or Arthur.

On the Third Day

And the Carpenter said 'I shall make a machine
that will filter the air clean of its poison;
that will pump and drag up water
from the deep rocks to the sky; a guardian of rainbows,
that will hold the soil steady, knotting it tight
with invisible, intricate webbing.
A machine that will surfeit a million insects,
hold the birds and the climbing tribes of apes;
a protection for my sons against wind and lightning,
a fuel that will heat their hands and faces;
whose by-products will be ships, and violins, and gallows;
whose shavings will be stained with my children's names,
their truths slowly discovered, their gorgeous lies,
their fingers' deftness with blue and gold and ochre.

My machine will cause poets to make verse,
will smell like honey and rain and ashes;
will break out yearly in a rash of apples;
will unleash a million berries.
I will call it oak, and beech and thorn;
I will design it in a thousand shapes and places,
and I will give it to my sons for their salvation
— let them guard it well.
On the day the sun dies and the rain is bitter
I will come and hang my sorrows from its branches.

Tapestry Room

The edge of the moon is unravelling.
Run your fingers down the clouds and brambles,
the soft, fraying silken owls.
Stags leap russet from a fungal forest
drained to a grey that drifts at the touch,
hanging on the spears of light thrust through it.

We breathe this in, it clogs our syllables,
tastes on our tongues; a skilled
fingerwork dissolving in our draughts.
Feel it on your skin, its faint
fur on your lips; see on the floor
how you've printed your pathway across it.

They all wove it, wove themselves into it,
a web of the tales and tellers
so we might loosen the woven hours like spore;
drifting out of themselves into rooms,
into echoes, into those who listen,
into a dust of moon and feathers in your voice and eyes.

Incident at Conwy

During the Wars of the Roses a Lancastrian officer was shot by a marksman stationed on the battlements of Conwy Castle. The river between them was at least half a mile wide. The feat was recorded by several chroniclers.

1. Llewelyn of Nannau

Oh man you are foolish to wear that surcoat.
The gold and the blue outrage the dull afternoon.
You are a heraldic flicker among the leaves
tempting my pride.
I have not killed men in the stench and fury
of battle only, that I would baulk at this.
I am an archer. I send death winging,
sudden and cold over parapet and fosse;
the lightning that strikes nowhere twice.
I'm too far away to see your pain,
the blood that will sully that bright coat;
too far for the shriek from your lady's arbour.
Nor will imagination spoil my aim.
The taut strings creaks against my fingers,
brushes my cheek softly, as I draw back.
My eye is steady down the shaven shaft.
You're a roebuck, a proud stag, a target.
Your words do not goad me, I can't hear what you say.
Your death will be skilfully given, and without rancour.
At least I am not too far from you for that.

2. Rhys ap Gruffudd Goch

The river is wide, and the leaves cover us.
We are safe enough, but they are certainly ready
— each tower and arrowslit is crowded with faces,
and notice the fool on the battlements with his bow.
This castle will drink an oblation of blood
before we break its stone teeth.

That archer has seen me; he lifts his bow.
Well the river will not bleed from his arrow.
Doubtless he would kill me if he could
and boast about it over the spilled wine;
a distant, stout, nameless man
who would never have seen my face.

Then he would thresh about in the straw at night,
seek solace from priests, drink away memory,
but the line would have been thrown between us,
the bright gift passed, that he could not take back.
Look, he draws. If he should strike me down
I will never be so far from him again.

In a Chained Library

Here they are, chained as if dangerous,
creatures from a bestiary left open,
foxed and gilded, a tangle of tails,
mouths, claws, spilling from the shelves.

Silent as unicorns their sweet unspoken music.
Finger them, the dry crackle of their skins.
Dragons burn in margins, sea-cats uncoil;
monsters, eating letters, being letters,

as if word and flesh and beast were one
and might burst out, huge and scaly,
slithering from the nave into the crowded streets,
scorching the night with a babel of lost songs.

Rose Flint

Rose Flint was born in London in 1944. After living for many years on the Welsh Borders she now makes her home in Bath. A writer and artist, she teaches creative writing to all age groups. Her broadcast poetry includes a *Kaleidoscope* special on the Isle of Man. Her Seren collection is *Blue Horse of Morning*.

Blue Horse of Morning

If I came to you now
on the blue horse of morning
how I would cackle the street bells
and set the ghosts groaning out of the light.
I could come as Cloud-Woman-Riding
shape myself into a message
over your roof. *Look, it is dawn,*
the winter is over, wanting is finished.
I have galloped the night-iron out
of our hooves. Accept this silver:
four bright moony hoops flung over the pole.

I could be cool, responding
to weathermen's turquoise oracles,
blue as the inside flame is blue.
You would know me as Ocean, lapping
your island back, fire-blue tiding up
through your heels to break kisses,
sparks over your neck, leave wet shadows.

Or choosing the warmth of lapis lazuli,
I would enter your dark troubled sleep
and thief-silent, go down to the place

where the black root twists darkness
into your dreams. Spreading the rustle
of indigo skirts I would open your mouth
with my long scented fingers
and place the sun on your tongue.

The Return of the Moth

The moths have returned.
Out of the shuttered clay
they come dizzying; pallor of wings
whir and creep on the slide of night glass,
eyes stud garnets desirous
to sip at our spill of light,
our spice room of fatal gold nutmeg.
Later, in May, the window glass
will clack and clatter with black Maybugs
hurling wing-jacket bodies,
urgent and careless
of thorax or precision filaments.

I am drunk with the moon's insect humming
the flare of sharp night-scent
new bulbs flower-swelling.
I could open this slit of a window
enter the vine, climb
down hand over hand, call you out:
Moth, Mothman —
the garden bending oak darkness over me;
my white body cold-grained as sugar
or salt, your old black coat
covering naked flame.

Brazen Marriage

After their love had brimmed the bed
and they had floated — dragonflies drowned
in their own heady amber — after he drowsed
into the tasselled cambric, her safe breasts

soft to his nuzzle and her long luxury of pliant bone
unrolled and owned by his momentary hands:
while he lay, a sleek curl in her stroking, netting fingers —
after that, she left him; slipped naked out of the sheets
to kneel on the Chinese ottoman under the window,
crushing dragon blooms of silk, fades of mandarin blossom.

On the other side of the glass
she watches the angels cluster, drift slowly down the hedgerow
through dusk or moonlight; their feet not quite touching
— or risking — the sharpness of quickthorn, mealy plum.
Recently their silvers have flushed to a faint hectic warmth
and one amongst them glistens, has taken the tint of soft metal,
red-gold or bronze. That was after she had lain differently,
her legs gentle hooks, the scarp of her husband's shoulders
a steep rapturous falling.
             This angel: his palms push down the light,
his half-skirts rustle impatiently, his penis — meek yet —
stirs in its golden skin. If this Lucifer
clapped his vast and brazen wings
the whole garden would shimmer and dance:
the wind of his feathers husking through oboes,
charming snakes. At his wish, English trees
would fruit with figs and pomegranates and the little foxes
find a sudden banquet of honeyed grapes to lick.
The kingfishers, bird and birdwife, would burn
blue flame down the darts of his eyes.

Turning back to the bed, she sees her husband's body lying open.
She trails her hands through the texture of his skin
feels his skin flow under and round her like waters,
senses its tensions, muscular wave motions.
Swimming in him, she lets him close over her head,
take her breathless, air becoming wine.
Watching her, his eyes go dark as water from earth-deep
as if she leaned into his eyes, the light behind her.
His body warms her garden scents and rain;
as her reflection fades from the glass.

Desmond Graham

Born in Surrey in 1940, Desmond Graham was educated at Leeds University. He has lectured in Africa, Germany and, since 1971, at Newcastle upon Tyne. He is the author of a biography of Keith Douglas and the editor of his poems and prose. He is also the editor of the Chatto anthology *Poetry of the Second World War*. His new Seren collection is *The Marching Bands* (1996).

from *Characters*

1. Leontes

He was pushing a pram up a hill
in a poorish district, talking
to the cushion plumped up inside.
He wore a suit too small for him,
frayed at collar and cuffs
and a little greasy.
He was alright, really;
just a bit abstracted.
Sometimes you saw him with a woman,
stockings round her ankles,
tottering in heels,
just a thin blouse
though it was winter.
They were walking down the same hill
with the same pram
with the cushion in it,
talking.

2. Lear

He carries everything he owns
about him, a toppling coat-stand,
overcoats humped on his back,
anoraks and jumpers
padding out his front
like a stage fat man.
He has a belt of washing line
hung with bags and bundles,
in each hand hold-alls and carriers
weigh him down. He moves like a boulder
in slow motion. No one bothers him,
not even children.
He says nothing.

3. Hamlet

He is tall and thin with stubble
and those spectacles snapped off
at one side and taped with plaster
over the nose-piece. The first time
I met him he was crying,
told me about his father,
could not be consoled:
to see a grown man in the street
dribbling and crying,
jacket stained with tears:
he lives round here,
I've seen him often since,
begging.

4. Macbeth

shadow boxes through the afternoons
in the covered market: he likes to do it
by the butcher's best: their great carcasses
hung up on gibbets, pigs' heads on a dish:
he'll be there, bobbing and feinting,

dabbing out an elbow, beer can in his fist:
and all the time a kind of talking,
gibberish in grunts and exclamations,
insults, invective, volleys of abuse
and not a word of sense among them:
the butcher boys put down their knives,
lean back and listen as he weaves on past,
another drop of shoulder, left jab, shuffle,
another burst of taunts, commands and threats,
none of it intelligible, nothing.

5. Lady Macbeth

Unbelievably in a shocking pink
mini, orange hair cropped,
no expense spared,
tiny as a ballerina
and past fifty,
green stilettos,
pale green stockings
and a lemon jacket,
brand new metal suitcase,
bags of make-up,
artificial sun-tan
she swung the case
to shoulder height
as anyone drew near
snarled a threat
and stared right through them
focussed,
terrifyingly,
on someone else not there.

6. Ophelia

Thank God for Ophelia
from the tower block
who survived them all
sane and seventy

or more, dancing
to the Juke Box
graceful as a Garbo,
with any man who cared
and had energy to match,
so long after
whatever fool
had shouted 'Time'.

At the Municipal Cemetery, Gdynia

Even in April the cold wind
lifts the skin off you and the hillside,
makes clear the absence of colour
as if after a fire
some mineral never got back;

the little red lights at the graves,
lamps for sanctuary far too late
to save dear ones, breathless
after that chase;

the flares stuck in the soil,
swirling a moment over their own light
like the dead now beneath them,
then swiftly gone into black.

The women bring handfuls of twigs in bud,
handfuls of overpriced flowers,
shared out like everything here
right through the family:

grandmother who never saw you,
uncle who loved you and nursed you
right through to his end, cousin
missed long after any way back,
and the lost still children.

This is the graveyard of bitterness,
of love's waste,
the breaths of pollution,
the price paid for too long a wait.

For Milena
(aged 2)

I would take you into my arms rolled up
like an astrolabe, ribbed and bound with love
impregnable and you would beat your hand prints
on the inside smoked, coming out like a chick's
beak or turtle tot, splitting my sides

I would take you into my bathysphere, well-cased
and rivetted to any depth, curling my whole weight
like nesting birds around you, hurdling you in
with tideless favour so the deep sea's swell
would be no more than breath on a window
blown for writing names, but you would crack
the embrasure, stride out like a new born armadillo
from its shell, bison worried at the water line,
porpoise from the net of sea, surfaced into air

I would hold you in a ring of talking soft enough
to suck cream with, spell all round the oaths
of surety which not a witch or gorgon
taking a brickbat stroll could launch through,
iron ribbed in feeling, haversacked in love,
safe from the outside and you would walk easy —
as you did from the first room with your eyes
slipping over mine to mother's and then on
to the great outside of walls and windows —
arms swinging, legs astride the world and moving,
your roller ball, into whatever.

Steve Griffiths

Steve Griffiths was born in Anglesey in 1949 where he lived until he was eighteen. He was educated at Cambridge and is the author of four collections, the most recent being 1993's *Selected Poems*. He lives in London where is is currently working as a freelance researcher in the fields of poverty, social security and local authorities.

The Mines in sepia tint

A man beats his wife on the mountainside.

Their shouts pierce the copper drumskin
of the coming storm: the earth of copper
the heather, the copper sky:

everything rumbles round inside the drum.

The man in a grey suit, white-faced,
his eyes shifting fast and nervous
copper copper copper copper the woman
outraged by my witness of her beating

my warning shout as I passed
and my feet pounded the veins of copper
across country: then, poised on thin white legs,
doubtfully angry, wet hair plastered on my forehead,
sixteen, not knowing what to do.

They gave me silent, heated looks,
and I ran on.

Later, I wrote a poem about the pylons on the horizon.

Often I have written the wrong poem.

Llangefni Market

1
The Bull

A black bull of enormous power
stands in its solitary pen
An inconceivable quantity of muscle
governs its mass.
It makes a bass, husky groan of sympathy
to a beef-cow in a nearby crowded enclosure,
throaty and demoralised, at the second attempt.
Its strong, gentle face: the black curls
of a solid Grecian deity.
The eyes of danger and deep water.
The mesmeric stillness, slow blinking.
We wonder at its marvellous career,
the balls slung low like footballs;
small townspeople shaken
by the industry of the carnivores, ourselves.
The rolling eyes of the smell of death.

A farmer passes, on first name terms with the bull.
It ignores him. He criticises the shortness of its legs.
I say, 'They've got a lot to carry', feeling ignorant.
'They won't have after today', he says with satisfaction,
and we walk away, to the next pen.

129

2
The Café

There are many great wellingtons in the café today,
a masculine air among the housewives.
A stockman sits beside us with a shy grin,
almost a sheep's mouth twist, full of teeth.
Blue eyes not right indoors, meant for wind.
He stares ahead, gripping his teacup
in his thumb, saying 'oh aye':
he twinkles into the middle distance.

A year ago today, it was all finished:
they fought the import of Irish cattle
when they could only give their own away
for the meaning of glut is disaster for them.
The farmer gets three times that price for beef now.
They changed the rules because of the song and dance.
'Oh aye, it's very good now' he nods
and swallows his tea to return to the market's rich smell.

Taking Shelter

a sensual heat on the heavy leaves
luxuriating Llaneilian under Mynydd Eilian

the church pricking the hard brightness of the summer
since Patrick walked this land, influencing leaders.

later the English appropriated the church
and the Welsh moved elsewhere, with such

items of culture they could carry.
still a heat of visions in the yellowing graveyard,

an overgrown place, for fornication.
the nave, a cool dark island:

a skeleton painted black on the twisted gallery
a small coffin at the foot of the tower

flutes and pipes in a glass museum case
shattered, something struck it,

the splinters in the aisle; the birds and myself
nervously stricken in the porch.

the stone flaking slowly at the gate
on other time-scales.

onrush of cars headed for the beach
the wind sways the bushes to silence

it is time to go down there slowly myself
the glass, dust, and rounded wood in my mind

and the painting of Eilian and his fixed eyes and his six
fingers, giver of power and a name to this place.

at the beach, my teeth sink delicately
in a Midnight Mint, turning it slowly on my tongue.

kids throw a ball over a sleeping labrador.
the full car park brighter than any sea.

looking at girls with their reddening legs
to dismiss them before they dismiss me.

walking home alone through the hawthorns.

Courage

My baby's harelip's darned brilliantly
like the hospital sheets he lies on.
Others wait for the train
back from the seventies,

where infant mortality grows
like a lump on the breast.

Wards close
and the nurses grow fierce, unnoticed.

Arms outspread in splints,
cherub or bird, his gums are bared
as his mother, his dependable
aviary of mobiles, and his father
move the other side of his tears.

His blood is bright as an old man's,
the incision part of my acute past.
Nerves run crying to my shoulder
when I think of it,
with an anxiety pale and grubby
as a sleepless father
wearing the badge of his lip
as he walks through my dream,
eyes and hands alight, chuckling
at his mother who leans over him
in a little storm of generosity.

The baby grins briefly
at his own strength
through his pain,
the first mirror.

Small substantial shadow

Our living proof that provokes the cat
to violence with love.

In a plastic mac with the sleeves turned up
he points at the rain
making dashes on the lake's dark screen.

Little maker and unmaker
his bed's a bazaar, like Pharaoh's tomb,
he can sleep on a book or a helicopter.

Little creator and destroyer,
he's our tender confluence
shouting and running in the hall:

a stone thrown out of our lives,
twisting away through the air
like a discus out of a stadium.

Our neighbours know it's the throwing,
the exuberant fling of the arm
with him, more than direction,

leaving the chaotic distant kisses blown,
rosepetals, the cigarpuff of a reporting gun.

Fluidity, Charmouth

A bare tree reaches over
from the cliff-edge mudslide:
dead of almost being airborne,
drawing up, drawing down
like a fishing rod,
a perch that has the air of carrion
for choughs that seethe up
from the marls below the lip.
Below, a skier on an avalanche,
there waits an ammonite
that glistens upward to the god's
eye that holds the scale of things.
The eye's blood-vessels
snag there in a branch.
A jug is pouring birds the other way.

Llantysilio, overgrown

Under the rush of caravans on the Holyhead road
and the thwack in the wind
of the campers' polythene streaming
and the hum of the scale-model traffic
on the miraculous bridges with realistic water below,
Tysilio's island hugs its cemetery to itself.

The graves are decked individually
as if each decomposition had its flower:
on dark slate, violet; the spindrift of the disappointed
lips cast from the cheekbone; and these delicate
heavenly ones, nodding at the mild Sunday air
after a lifetime stamped in the gasping furrow.

A green-armed bramble
lances the wind on a thousand tiny fronts
for the unremembered improvisor of hovels,
for tillers and singers, the little stone-skimmers:
a voice secreted over the mouths stained
with their own juices in their made beds.

Glyndŵr Subdued

Burned out, there was no road back,
and the flames of Sycharth brought Glyndŵr
dreams enough:
his home was a country now,
the revenges multiplied.
The helicopter's shadow,
a great hare
runs fleetingly across a field —
the grass panicking, flattened,
trying to disperse but unable.

Almost an experiment,
the disciplined ructions of the first raid,
the strained respect for brawny lives
a delicate line: Rhuthun settlers,

robbed and dishevelled, emerged
to a heady, bright, small Welsh triumph
reeking of sheepshit
and soot in the bright sun:

insults counted, it was a homely,
small, scared, village altercation
as shoving and grunting skirmishes
around slag once made history.

The victors clattered away
shod heavily with expensive curses
to where even the sparks on the hill
were drunk down by the mud and the dark.

Later the conscripts, cast-off and dangerous,
sported their rusted dream of omnipotence,
hacking for their neglected fields
and their friends cut down,

and then for the riven cold in their bones
women ran in the wet grass
brought down like deer with cries of triumph.
People ran blindly,

made his, the pervasive guerilla
reeking of smoke and prophecy,
the peaceloving fire
displaced in his rafters.

The banging of shields,
plastic and leather,
rang in his ears:

war war war sle sle sle
went the childish wailing of sirens
in the gusting wood,

and the night's drunken instruments
scoured the wet streets
for the Welsh doggis and their whelps.

An English city listens behind curtains
to the running and breathing, the slugging
thud of quarry cornered and floored:

the resistance is
that we will not turn the television up
in tribute to the night.

Divided loyalties, undermined
meal-tickets, sprouted on hillsides,
the weeds Indignation
twined with deep-rooted Ambivalence

picked for the same dish.
Drenched resisters sidled in droves
along valleys to give themselves up
to the straggling columns of troops and grain.

When the fighting is over, the land of dreams
is a table lit with unshareable faces,
a once-in-a-lifetime
remembered meal to the hungry:

a looted peacock under the arm
of some big, sharp-featured
father of mine
who dried his eyes at the flame of Sycharth.

Then the withdrawal to memory
of the fair people, walled in the clouds
of exile within, the retreat to mystery
of the fair times on their vague upland tracks.

Glyndŵr had to master this potent
trick of retirement, to the light
in a dolmen glimpsed rarely and late,
a light in the mind

where sometimes he lingers noisily in the grid of years
and the speed and charisma growl in him
to the applause of the shingle in the undertow,
old chimera whose wait has a tide's hypnotic

push still. It breaks
in like the sudden clatter of leaves
of a kneeling army

or a belief in the mountains upturned,
with mirrors,
lit from inside with our own light.

(The poem uses the chant of the northern English students at
Oxford, heard by Adam of Usk, at the beginning of the Glyndŵr
uprising:

War war war, sle sle sle
the Welsh doggis and their whelps.)

Paul Groves

Paul Groves was born in 1947 in Gloucester and brought up in Wales. He has taught for many years, read at arts centres, festivals and on the radio, and been successful in national and international poetry competitions. His second Seren collection, *Ménage à Trois*, appeared in 1995. He currently lives with his family in the Forest of Dean.

All Hallows' Eve

The heads of antelopes adorn the walls.
Their plastic eyes have witnessed savagery
as meals were disembowelled and wines decapitated
with the sound of buckshot. The captain
stalks these walks, a living ghost dedicated
to the butchery of flowers he crams in vases
adorned with sea-shells older than civilization.
His monocle steams up at the thought of squid
waiting for the sea-caves of his stomach,
Montrachet thick as blood, and pastries
aborted from the hands of the hirsute chef.
Guests will arrive soon, women with dresses
revealing a winkle navel, men who sell
armaments to developing Third World nations.
The servants are decked in the livery
of hand-picked angels from the castle's gardens:
their cheeks are from the orangery, and for eyes
lavender has been culled without superstition.

It promises to be a memorable ball; the speeches
will live on, trapped in the rafter's cobwebs
like beautiful flies, as the crab-like spiders move
delicately across their traceries of lace.

Anniversary Soak

What kind of love is this when she
Lifts down the urn from its high place
And takes the top off gingerly
As if about to see his face,

And then rolls down her stockings as
She did that first night they were wed,
While he lay back there, bold as brass,
A bronzed young god upon the bed?

What sort of memory is kept
Alive as both the taps are turned?
That marriage day they never slept
But like two endless fuses burned.

She steps into the swirling heat,
Uncertain whether she should stoop
Or kneel; she looks down at her feet,
And tips the ashes in. The soup

That greyly laps her limbs is him,
The only man she ever craved,
The only one to keep her warm,
With whom alone she misbehaved.

Forgetting Water

It took a lifetime to remember it,
to avoid it when something chucked it
out of the skies, or when it lay around
in ambushing puddles. It took a lifetime

to clean your teeth with it. And then,
Father, I saw you relinquish the concept
of water. You jettisoned it with so
much else: furniture, religious beliefs,
the facts of life. You died like a man
who had nothing, a deposed emperor,
some desperate hobo slumped on a park bench,
a bishop who is longing to hear angels
but senses only his housekeeper's unhelpful cough.
You were spared most ironies and paradoxes:
you died simply, like a fire deprived
of anything to feed on. You took with you
what you thought of me, what you remembered
of our years together. No wonder people drink
to excess, adulterize, drive recklessly.

Greta Garbo

*A Japanese paparazzo photographer has been waiting outside her
apartment for more than three years, but has never succeeded in
getting a full-face picture.*

Mostly you get the din of the Franklin D. Roosevelt Drive,
traffic plying this throughway beside
the East River. Mostly you get the sense
of being alive, of being five time zones from home,
from that family rooftree in Kawasaki, one block
from the Sojiji Temple. I have captured
kids playing pat-ball at one two-fiftieth of a second
at f4, leaves drifting to the ground on East 52nd
at proportions of that speed, but
Dame Fortune stays elusive. For thirty-eight months
she has not bought zucchini. I find this remarkable.
The Americans call a swede a rutabaga;
I call this Swede the whole vocabulary,
depending on my mood: witch, goddess, foil, mantrap.
It is as if she never lived, and all I have done
for a slice of my life is kick cans,
light up another Lucky Strike, hope yet again

to strike lucky. I suppose this is an odyssey
in pursuit of elusiveness itself, a quest
for the resurrection of beauty: Odysseus
blew a decade on his errand. There's time yet.
When the wind blows, desperate, down from Maine,
and it's thirty below, I curse and stamp
and spend all day in the diner, wiping
condensation from the pane, focusing.
He brings me soup, and tuts, scratching his head.
'I thought Polacks were the limit, but
you're something else.' Life has become
a philosophical acceptance of loss, a conflation
of zilch and Zen. Something stirs,
but it is only the janitor humping garbage
onto the sidewalk for the next collection.
She made a movie called *Joyless Street*
in 1925, the year my mother was born
high in the hills near Kawakami
where the snowflakes are huge, and the air silent.

The Back End of the Horse

Was it a phoney coin that let
Him be the upright part, the eyes,
For two years running? It's damned hot
And dark down there: his hips and thighs,
My forehead on his buttocks. Pain
Will gnaw my back and neck again

This pantomime. Blindly I'll shuffle,
Kicking the air — a carefree colt,
While really I begin to stifle,
Dripping with acrid beads of sweat.
The better I perform the more's
The likelihood that the applause

141

Gets transferred to the brainy part,
My partner in this dumb charade.
He has the conscience and the heart,
The massive teeth, the fun facade;
I have the stumbling, shambling gait,
The lifeless tail, the clumsy feet.

His mane is stroked; my rump is slapped.
His mammoth eyelashes seem coy,
Endearing; and he is adept
At smooching with the leading boy.
An ugly sister boots my rear.
Oh, which is worse: the pain or fear?

An analyst would know, I think,
Why I allow myself this pressure.
Is it a masochistic kink,
Finding in suffering some pleasure,
Euphoria in obscurity?
A man of straw. It sounds like me.

A stable relationship? Perhaps.
We need each other, fore and aft.
We do not care if other chaps
Suppose our thespianism daft.
We may not be a thoroughbred
— I may feel stupid and half dead —

But *something* makes this seem worthwhile.
Cynics could trot out Jung and Freud
To underpin their canny smile
And clarify my hopeless void.
Let them. Lost, I blunder on
Until the entertainment's done.

Eduardo on a Scooter

There is nothing to do, and he is doing it.
His heart beats for this.
His engine purrs with pleasure.
All moving pieces are well oiled.
His hair is slick, as is his manner
— yet he is not insincere.
'Ti amo,' he says, as much to his Vespa
as to you; or perhaps he expresses love
for the face in the mirror,
sunset on the Tiber....
There are so many shining surfaces:
the chrome of his machine,
the sheen of his sunglasses.
Viale Trastevere is vibrant.
The air takes on new coolness
after the oxyacetylene day.
Has he read that *La Republica*
stuffed into his oxblood bomber jacket?
Does he use expensive dentifrice
for so effulgent a grin?
Are those restorer's hands,
as able to touch up an old painting
as a young woman?
Instantly I regret my English upbringing.
Seldom were we so carefree in the shires.
Rarely did life light up
in such surprising colours.
He may not get rich.
He may grow fat and fortyish
in the high-rise suburbs,
but, for the moment, he is Adonis,
on the verge of the street and a new conquest,
bright, almost invincible.

The Torturer's Coffee

He slumps onto a cane chair, tired
though it is not yet noon, pushes back
the white, blood-flecked baseball cap,
sighs. A colleague throws a packet of cheroots.
The recipient grunts in appreciation.
On the verandah a child triggers a toy gun.
Here under Capricorn cool dry days are as rare
as an unforced confession. Mostly a little
coercion is needed. Techniques vary
with the individual. At dawn he shoots
birds out of the trees. He hates their freedom,
their communistic excesses.
Order must be imposed. The junta decrees it.
The coffee is as black as hate. Hate is good.
It enables him to work professionally.
Women are not his line. Alfredo
deals with them; he has the knack —
he uses the barbed wire like an artist.
Carlos is consummately able with a syringe;
while José's a madman: give him a scissors
and he coos like a baby.
A reporter arrived three weeks ago,
some trailblazing city liberal
grubbing for clues about the CIA.
He should have been a bird at dawn
then he would have received his answer.
'*Cia* as in *estancia* would that be?'
Suddenly it's back to work. Maintaining files
is a chore, but information
must be logged. Each scream could lead to
new addresses, names, an uptown number
or someone down the long dirt road
who needs a salutary visit.

Ultima Thule

An initial result of Eskimo contact with whites was the
Floradora Sextet, an amateur cancan line of native girls.

Number One is not used to the smoke. Eyes get
bejewelled with tears. She keeps smiling.
Number Two is fascinated by the intestines
of the trombone. It glints like narwhal tusks.
Number Three is, as usual, taciturn. She dances,
according to the Yank impresario, like an elephant.
This leaves her nonplussed. What is an elephant?
Number Four is the baby of the party. At thirteen
she is even less able to differentiate art from tomfoolery.
Number Five is Number Two's sister. She, at seventeen,
is having her first period. She feels like whalemeat.
Number Six has devised their routine. It entails
showing strange southerners underclothes in the name
of Terpsichore. The introduction of camiknickers
is a Greek gift. No such garment suits the ampleness
for which local women are renowned. High cheekbones.
Twelve left feet. An aurora borealis of petticoats.
The hall fills up: men desperate for release
from cold celibacy, enforced exposure to a lack
of Boston or Sacramento. The ivories are vamped,
a flenching of doubt, as certainty strides centre stage.
'Gentlemen...'. He speaks with force but without conviction.
'The Cream of the Arctic, the Passion Flowers
of Prudhoe Land — I give you, for your delectation...'.
Number Three has to be dragged forward into the wings.
Her inflamed face aches in the mirror. 'Floradora,'
she says, her mouth full of stones. 'What do we *mean*?'

Mike Haines

Mike Haines was born in London in 1948. He moved to Anglesey in 1970 and taught English before becoming an HMI in 1986. He now lives in Cardiff and works in schools and colleges across Wales. Current weaknesses include: hostas, hardy geraniums, lost and forgotten plays. His Seren volume is called *The Seeds of Things*.

Transylvanian Romance

Nothing
is more frightening
than the face of fear.
The Count's agonized grimace
(given our young couple's presence
of mind to fix
him with a crucifix)
more worrying
than any lewd and threatening
leer.

Girls,
of course,
hearing the stairs creak,
must shriek
at their devouring father's
forbidden advance. But as for us,
we sympathize
when sunrise
finds him safe again
in his coffin's silk-lined sanctuary.

We recognise
        the malevolence built into
this celluloid cosmology
        where mirrors,
        cheated of reflection,
                prove
        flesh an illusion.

        Where
a stake through the heart
(inescapable denouement)
        sets in motion
        that hideous
and instantaneous withering
        of muscle and skin
through which the bones of the undead
        shine.

        Finally leaving behind
        only empty caskets
                which
        like craters
are the scars of catastrophe.

And what of the lovers?
        She, coy and domestic,
        rescued in the race
which is always against time,
        the just reward
        of his insipid optimism.

        For the connubial couple,
so inauspiciously united,
        time must for ever after roll
        uninterestingly
        by.

Soft Fruit

Dictatorships rise and fall
    like hare-brained barometers;
in air-conditioned committee rooms
    the merchants of war
are consulting the FT Index.
    And I am wasp-dodging
in the gooseberry bushes,
    delicately negotiating
the hooks and claws, lifting
    the spitefullest branches
weighed down with burst berries
    which fill a sticky fist —
then back to the kitchen
    for topping and tailing.

Police reinforcements
    have been called up;
helmeted behind riot shields
    they prepare for the baton-charge;
embarrassed scabs are bussed
    into pits through pickets
waving clenched fists.
    Flickering beside the pond
dragonflies still hover
    in the late sun's slanting rays;
the last raspberries, slipped
    off their cauliflower cores
and sprinkled with castor sugar,
    are frozen on trays.

Tetchy behind tinted windscreens,
    cabinet ministers refuse comment;
commentators are agonizing
    through action replays,
and on victory rostra, sporting
    their medals, Olympians
are sobbing through anthems.

I am moving into the currants;
easily stripping the red, they go
        pattering into the bowl;
teasing the fat black ones
        from their stalks — the ripest
leaving their hearts behind, staining
        my fingers with stubborn blood.

Paul Henry

Paul Henry was born in Aberystwyth in 1959. Originally a singer-songwriter, he has degrees in English and Drama and currently combines freelance writing with his work as a Careers Advisor. He received an Eric Gregory Award in 1989. He currently lives in Newport, Gwent with his family. *Captive Audience*, his second Seren collection, appeared in 1996.

Widows of Talyllyn

They lived as needed, hid their strength,
survived the male, modestly,

block the aisle on the market bus,
still see husbands in summer fields,

still wear rings on mortal fingers,
grasp cupfuls of chipped memories,

wake at sober dawns and leave
their precious days unsquandered.

Trevor's
i.m. T.C. Thomas, playwright 1896-1989

Old man, it was a broad sun
peeling off at Pen-y-Fan,
the lambing mostly done,
almost Spring at Heddfan.
Still winter at your collar

made the nursery touch-and-go,
the orchard a frail distiller
of dusk, the bland hedgerow
unpromiscuous.
A chill set in.

This now, posthumous,
as much for the grandson
home to you gone
as for your simple crop of plays.
But if they plant a stone
in Llanfihangel or Llangorse
it will be good, your name
weathering out, a word or two
('A bit of a boy in his time'?)
underneath, it will do.

Busker

Chagall's black-eyed violinist
is busking outside Saint David's Hall,
blue-handing Irish jigs to the air,
to the mad hats of a serious town, gulls
in a shabby perfection of flight
above the Hayes Island snack-bar.
The tune shivering on is the one
another fiddler used to play
and I bow down to the open case
in the manner of taking, not giving,
of placing an ear to a cold stone
and catching the tail end
of a river that went underground.
Taken for granted in full spill
somewhere steeply greener than here.

It surfaces now, snatches at feet
and fills an empty pocket of time
with a currency of belonging.

As out of his hands again, the wild
ignited flock
will not stop dancing overhead,

will not stop dancing, minutes after
the slim shadow man,
in search of another precinct,
slackens and slips out of sight.

Comins Coch

Coming in from the yard, we unlearnt
the natural dance of play, stiffened
into rows, one for each class, hands
reaching to touch the shoulder in front,

to establish neat spaces. Miss Jones,
our referee, after the shuffled pack
took order, would double-check
her game of patience on the linear stones.

She once broke the cane on Emyr Brees,
set him homework to cut another
from his father's hedge. Quiet Heather's
tears ran down her knees.

On the canteen wall, Sir Ifan ap
Owen M. Edwards, above the sprouts
and gooseberries, turned away, motes
of the alphabet caught in his sun-trap.

Time spelt up right. We got xylophones,
slide-rules, projector-screens,
trips to Chester Zoo and St. Fagans,
a topic on Ghana's coffee beans.

Miss Jones started to smile. The smell
of swede from the kitchen grew tame.

I pulled on the ring of the steel frame
so the field hung at an angle

in the huge window all afternoon,
waiting for the bell. We discussed,
in English: Carlo, George Best
and the next Apollo. The blackboard spun.

With her back to us, that last Friday,
with her bucket, her housecoat over her dress,
she might have been polishing glass,
not square, chalk-marked infinities.

Museum Café

This is their tomb to smile in,
the cream-trousered Englishmen.
They are important it seems.
Their teacups are megaphones.

Ignoring the girl who serves them,
(her presence might be some fleck
of native soil on excavated china),
their tongues connect with bits of French.

And we who should speak louder
are just another meal between digs,
artefacts, documented only by
the occasional nervous glance.

This much will remain,
outside of the silence,
when they exit, full-bellied,
off to bigger countries —

remnants on the side of a plate,
the boneshape of a dinosaur.

Fatherless Friends

Like untopped ferns they grew absurdly tall,
swayed on touchlines while others chased a ball,

crossed their legs and frowned ahead of their time.
To one, theft was the only natural crime.

Now he builds homes while another interprets dreams
and a third dissects pianos in empty rooms.

Odd reunions bring their gentle beards
towering over my boyish smile, their cords

worn at the knees and, almost fatherly,
their massive, priestly hands, protecting me.

At This Hour

'Some now are happy in the hive of home,
Thigh over thigh and a light in the night nursery...'
Louis MacNeice (*Autumn Journal II*)

A neighbour ventures out to paint his gate.
Cars open and close the acts of dreams.
The cleansing properties of the estate
get to work, begin to seep at the seams:

Arms and feet slip through the bars of their cots.
A sigh lets love go at last.
Ties forget themselves, out of their knots.
Someone else's egg is forecast.

Another black hole waits to be starred.
You turn on your side and the bed slides to the wall.
The soul of a house groans behind its facade.
Moon-struck roofers rehearse how to fall.

The Sorting Office factory-farms the mail.
Sealed eyes read up on how to cry.
Glazed marriages hang by a single nail.
The paint on the brilliant gate starts to dry.

154

Joyce Herbert

Joyce Herbert was born in 1923 in the Rhondda and read English at University College, Cardiff. She has published poems, short stories and had plays broadcast on the radio. Her Seren volume is called *Approaching Snow*. She is currently working on new poems and translations.

Dossers at the Imperial War Museum

A place devoted to death. At noon, when I came out, the sun
struck at my eyes. I'd been trying to hear Minnenwerfers,
catch the flare of a Verey light, the thud of a phosgene shell.

Across one wall a blinded daisychain of men went clambering
like stricken insects waving feeble antennae. Eyes burnt out,
they clutched the jacket of the man in front:
this neat clean dugout never knew them, neither did
the model soldier standing at the door, his webbing blancoed,
boots bright, puttees perfect, head high.
A general's delight.

There were photographs of running figures wavering,
lurching, buckling at the knees. There were humped heaps
fallen, stranded like fish on a desolate beach.

Sunshine showered sparks, drenched the steps.
I could not see, shaded my eyes.
They were all out there. Some tide of war had washed them
down the steps from Bapaume or the Somme,
rolled in cocoons of blankets, sprawled on their backs, knees up,

155

spilled on the shaven grass:
prone near the flowerbeds they slept like stones,
jaws dropped, mittened fingers clutching.
Far under bushes I could see them
in attitudes of death,
rolled in their plastic bags waiting for something to happen.

Approaching Snow

Snow is near. Already small insects climb the walls of sheds,
the stars have sunk in space, threads of light,
silence is running like ice along the air.

Coming in this year of my life to the house of my parents,
I think of the others who may still be here,
and of all the animals and insects on this hill,
I am for them, they are for me.

Snowclouds are stretching in bands of grey across the woods,
the colour of industrial smoke.
The earth is cooling down.

Snow will push against the house many times,
but the seams will hold.
Quivering under it, the seeds and the hidden animals
wear it on their backs in a dark sleep.

The house is a lighted ship under the crawl of clouds,
the last birds lift and fall to safety,
quarrel beneath branches.

Some of them will be fighting after the thaw:
the washed house will shine.

Experience behind Headley Church

The land sags away
behind the church,
a sudden cornfield standing thick,
white, just before turning, sown
in martial drills sprung into line.

Stopping, we look down over it,
flung like a savage efflorescence,
white bristles turning ochre privately, steadily.

There's a path like a spear thrown straight,
it parts machine-sown stalks.
Dry, strong, rattling,
stiff as a stablebrush, ramming the solid in phalanxes,
they cover all.

We walk in a world of wheat.
The wind fingers it. No stalk bends.
A black dog runs down from the church.
He is grinning.
He is also wet to the skin. He stares at us.
He passes silently.

A crow flaps out of the solid corntop.
The movement releases us as if a key is turned.
We advance.

Quivering, hissing,
the corn is indifferent to us,
the undulating extent of it
moving into the trees of the horizon
is troubling, like a drum.
Behind us it closes in.
We are growing in the forty acres
and a combine will collect us
when our time comes.

Lucien Jenkins

Born in 1957 in England, Lucien Jenkins was educated at Cambridge and London Universities. He has translated the poetry of Rilke and Baudelaire as well as edited the *Collected Poems* of George Eliot. He is currently editor of *Early music today* magazine in London where he lives with his family. He is a Welsh speaker.

The Hanged Men

Your heads on one side like thoughtful children
and hands behind your back quite thoughtfully,
you hang in rows.

Always the onlookers, part audience
part congregation, stand expressionless
in their cheap suits,

while men in uniforms and caps, who try
to look as if they know a thing or two,
look serious,

hoping to persuade us that a man hung
in a tree is quite normal, quite clever.
Pleased with themselves

they seem happy to place this achievement
on record. Will they send the picture home
to be hung up?

Perhaps they think it is a work of art,
this man in a badly pollarded tree.
Meanwhile the line

grows longer and the dreaming, floating world
in which they drift like mobiles will not wake.
The audience,

gathered like drifting leaves, seem unsurprised
and unalarmed. The wind blows. They scatter,
light as ashes.

Less

The Earth shrank slowly at first,
Early reports were suppressed
and the rumours not believed.

All carried on as before.
The Earth's anorexia
seemed to alarm nobody.

As the shrinking continued
things were closer together.
Open space was hard to find.

When Warsaw met Leningrad
everyone tried to behave
as if this were quite normal.

In Japan it was agreed
that if everyone stood still
none would fall into the sea.

In the Atlantic, fishing
boats found themselves run aground.
Cross channel ferries were squashed

as the channel grew slimmer.
Territorial disputes
arose as nations withered.

159

Then the pace quickened.
Gravity grew less.

Things started falling.
Oxford Street got lost.

The attempt was made
to tie down Heathrow

but the cables snapped.
The sky became full

of objects falling
away from the Earth.

Then it was noticed
nothing had been heard

from France for some time.
Whole populations

simply disappeared.
The last survivors

desperately tried
to keep holding on

but the earth
now the size

of a plum
escaped them.

As they fell
they could see

the debris
of the shrunk

Earth, slowly
spinning round.

The Eye

Something made his eye catch fire
one day on his way to work.
Flames leapt out and scorched his face.

Passers-by saw it happen.
'Gracious!' they said. 'Do you see?
That man's left eye is on fire.

Whatever next? I must say —
one's eye on fire in the street —
it's indiscreet, don't you think?'

All the way to work he saw
people nudge one another.
He ignored the whole affair.

Something must have caught his eye,
something inflammatory.
Once ablaze it would not douse.

At work he concentrated
while his forehead was melting:
he refused to be sidetracked.

He flicked through the day's reports
with attention to detail.
His assistant seemed upset.

His whole head was a bonfire.
A decision was needful.
But he delayed, hanging fire.

Mike Jenkins

Mike Jenkins was born in Aberystwyth in 1953. He was educated at the University of Aberystwyth and has taught in Northern Ireland and Germany. He currently lives in Merthyr Tudful with his family where he works as a writer, teacher and co-editor of The Red Poets' Society magazine. Author of five Seren collections, his most recent book is *This House, My Ghetto* (1995).

Chartist Meeting
Heolgerrig, 1842

The people came to listen
looking down valley as they tramped;
the iron track was a ladder
from a loft to the open sea —
salt filling the air like pollen.

Each wheel was held fast
as you would grip a coin;
yet everything went away from them.
The black kernel of the mountains
seemed endless, but still in their stomachs
a furnace-fire roared,
and their children's eyes hammered
and turned and hollowed out a cannon.

Steam was like a spiral of wool
threaded straight down the valley,
lost past a colliery.
The tramways held the slope
as though they were wood of a pen.

Wives and children were miniatures
of the hill, the coal engrained
in enclosures on their skin.

They shook hands with the sky,
an old friend; there, at the field,
oak trees turned to crosses
their trunks bent with the weight
of cloud and wind, and harsh grass
from marshes that Morgan Williams,
the weaver, could raise into a pulpit.

A thousand listened, as way below them
Cyfarthfa Castle was set like a diamond
in a ring of green,
and the stalks of chimneys
bloomed continuous smoke and flame.

The Welsh that was spoken
chuckled with streams, plucked bare rock,
and men like Morgan Williams
saw in the burnt hands a harvest of votes.

A Truant

Looking down on the open-cast pit,
a black crater, with tracks coiled
like an electrical circuit,
and yellow trucks like remote-controlled toys.
Sheer cliff blasted out has given
the mountain many spasms of shock.

With biscuit tin for his companion, we meet him,
the nightwatchman. Where he lived the nettles
and bracken root out the foundation.
His words lay bare the seam below our feet,
obstinate coal which can touch men like a plague —
the moonscape recedes beneath his peaked cap.

As if there were no fences or danger signs
he invites us to enter, as if the whole mountainside
were his parlour. He tells of pensioners
trying to hide behind the winter dark
as they snuffled out lumps of coal —
let them home along the path in his own boot-prints.

'Welsh lagoons there!' he says, 'even the weeping
of the dead miners is black'. I look again
at the bush-browed ponds of pumped water,
to Aberdare in the pocket of the hills
and then at the man, out whinberry-picking,
a truant from the narrow streets of the town.

Reflection in a Reservoir

It was a time of light
that a camera would have to be patient
as a fisherman to catch:
the church spires of conifers
and the brick-colour of larch
suddenly drowned in the valley.

Somehow, in the reflection I expected
to see the spires brought to earth
and changed into sturdy chapels
(once barns that stored Welsh)
and the larches to be stretched
into a village street of a past century.

But the water was soon made metal,
a dark-grey coin they melted down
to be dammed by minds in offices
where it was weighed. Would it become
the colour of coal by night-time?

from *Empire of Smoke*
Memorials

There are men with rising-damp in their bones,
men with germs working double-shifts and overtime
in their veins, men whose mouths
could outdrink their brains,
whose hearts sack the rest of their bodies.

There are women about to give birth
to washing-machines, women whose blue-mould
bruises are painted over with make-up,
who take pills because of chronic discrimination,
who catch cancer from watching too much television.

I came here looking for an answer to sleep —
my mind at nights travelling into exile.
Will they sever the trail
from the stomach of the Depression?
Will they stitch up the deep cuts
left when thousands had to leave this town?

They built a warehouse of graves
in Pant, to store the bodies which had been
dipped into the stench-filled crucible
of Lord Cholera's finest possession.

What memorial will we have?
Streets named after Dic Penderyn and Wellington
squaring up both sides of the valley
alive only with wandering dogs?

Industrial Museum

Hello and welcome to our industrial museum.

On your right there's a slag-heap reclaimed...
a hill... another slag-heap...

165

that one shaped as a landing-pad
for bird-like hang-gliders.

Notice the pit-wheels perfectly preserved
where you can buy mementoes
of the Big Strike and eat authentic cawl
at an austere soup-kitchen.

There mummified miners cough and spit
at the press of a button
and you can try their lungs on
to a tape-recording of Idris Davies' poems.

That rubble was a 19th century chapel,
that pile of bricks an industrial estate.
The terraced houses all adorned
in red, white and blue as if royalty were visiting.

See how quaint the wax models
of women are, as they bow in homage
to polished doorsteps, the stuffed sheep
at the roadside give off a genuine odour.

The graveyards have been covered over
and lounge-chairs provided for viewing
gravestones which tell of deaths from cholera
or pit explosions. I recommend their cafeterias.

In the ruins of the Town Hall the council
give public performances, meeting
to discuss the valley's future:
their hwyl is high and hiraeth higher.

Finally, let's visit the Foot Arms
(in memory of a long-gone leader)
and listen to the last Valley's character
who lives here, courtesy of the Welsh Office, in a tin bath.

Canine Graffiti

Some loopy boy wrote 'FUCK OFF'
in firm felt-tip on the white back
of a nippy-as-a-ferret Jack Russell.

Senior Staff spotted it while it shat
in the midst of a modern dance
formation — leotards snapped!

(When they weren't busy piercing ears
with sharp instructions, or spiking hair
with swift backhand cuffs,

they did have time to snoop on lessons
which exceeded the statutory decibel rate.)
They set off in pursuit of the errant dog,

skilfully hurdling its poop in the process.
They chased it into Mathematics
where it caused havoc by lifting a leg

45° towards the blackboard's right-angle.
Then through the Audio-Visual concepts room,
across the film of *Henry V,* making Olivier's horse

rear and throw the bewildered actor.
It hid behind a smoke-screen in the bogs,
sniffed out bunkers in the coal-bunker.

For hours it disappeared and Senior Staff
suspected a trendy English teacher
of using it as an aid to creative writing.

Finally it was duly discovered
by Lizzie Locust (Biology), necking
with a stuffed stoat in the store-cupboard.

Now you can see the distraught Headmistress
scrubbing from bell to bell in her office,
a small dog held down by burly, sweating prefects.

Creature

Last night the sea heaved up a creature,
one I could not explain.

Half-boat, half-animal it seemed:
ribs of rusted tin, skull smooth as plastic.

My daughter played in its house of bones,
bouncing pebbles like syllables ringing.

She kept asking its name, how old was it?
Was it a dragon? Oil like blood dripped.

'I don't know!' I said (sounding unscientific):
she pulled out bolts of its neck to sit on.

I pursued it in books: the Bible dumb.
She ran in and out of its tunnel of questions.

Famous Player

Larger than television
he'd drink anyone
under the floor,
gathered around him
like family and fire,
waiting on every word
the smell of scandal
stronger than draught beer:
a holiday and setting fire
to women's knickers
the team behaving just like
any other slobby trippers,
obsessed with the size of plonkers
and dubious strikers
who could go either way.
The chairman's an asset-stripper,

the manager's his dummy,
but he's City till he leaves
to sell his kicks
across the market-fields.
He talks fan-lingo
he was there when it 'went off'
at Bristol, as though
the fighting were a bomb
someone else had planted.
He's bigoted then liberated
spitting 'bent' and 'racist'
in a single sentence,
shrunk in his shoes
we just begin to argue
as he gets up to go.

Gurnos Shops

An emaciated tree
clinging to its blackened leaves,
the wind snuffles chip-cartons.

The road's an aerial view
of dirt-dragging streams,
its scabs peeled off by tyres.

Clouds collect exhaust-fumes.
A man takes his beer-gut for a walk,
his wife follows on a lead unseen.

They won't climb up on plinths
where benches ought to be
and pose like shop-dummies.

Lamp-posts droop their nightly heads,
strays will do the watering.
Graffiti yells, but nobody's listening.

Nigel Jenkins

Born in Gower in 1949, Nigel Jenkins has studied film and literature at Essex University and travelled extensively in Europe, Africa and Asia. He has worked as a newspaper reporter, lecturer and writer. A Welsh learner, he still lives in Gower. His most recent book is *Gwalia in Khasia* (Gomer) an account of Welsh missionaries in India. *Song and Dance* is his single Seren volume.

First Calving

Up through the rain I'd driven her, taut
hocks out-sharing a streak of the caul,
and that single hoof, pale as lard,
poked out beneath her tail.

In shelter,
across the yard from me now,
her rump's whiteness fretted the dark.
I watched there the obscure passage
of men's hands and, exiled in crass
daylight, waited —
       till a shout
sent me running big with purpose
to the stable for a halter.

They flipped to me the rope's end, its
webbing they noosed around the hoof:
we leaned there, two of us, lending weight
to each contraction; the other fumbled
for the drowning muzzle, the absent leg,

170

said he'd heard that over Betws way
     some farmer'd done this with a tractor —
          pulled the calf to bits and killed the cow.

Again she pushed, and to first air
we brought the nostrils free; next the head
and blockaging shoulders, then out
he flopped, lay there like some bones pudding
steaming with life.

                    Later,
she cleansed. I grubbed a hole in the earth
and carried the afterbirth out
on a shovel: to be weighted with a stone,
they said, to keep it from scavengers.

               The Ridger

     Capsized, by some nosing cow,
     in the headland where last unhitched,
     it raises to the solitudes
     guide-arm, wing and wheel.

     What should slide or spin
     locks to the touch; a bolt-head
     flakes like mud-slate at the push
     of a thumb — fit for the scrapyard
     or, prettified with roses, some
     suburban lawn. Yet there persist,
     in a tuck away from the weather,
     pinheads of blue original paint.

     To describe is to listen, to enter
     into detail with this ground
     and this ground's labour; to take
     and offer outward continuing fruit.

     My palm smoothes the imperfect chill
     of rusted iron... I weigh against
     the free arm, easing up

                    171

the underside share — worms retire,
lice waggle away: it stands
on righted beam, rags of root-lace
draped from the delivered haft.

Maker and middleman emblazon
two cracked plaques: Ransomes, Ipswich;
White Bros., Pontardulais.
Less patent is the deeper tale
that gathers with the touch of rain
on the spike which was a handle,
the nail bent over for an axle-pin.

Field on a Cliff

Devonian red, slabbed sheer
from the sea, tipping to light
   this patch of ruled hay.

Swathes down, hair parted; swathes
over, the flash-grey of severed nerves
   rippling all
      through the heat.

Was this morning cut
and, given the sun, will be carried
by nightfall tomorrow.

And here in winter, on this top
which lay once deep beneath waves,
      returning waves,
will cattle, of the field's return, be fed.

They'll spread for the herd
the warmth of old hay that lies now
liquid in the late June air,
         each bale as it breaks
         exhaling dust
         through the breath of fat steers.

Kate Johnson

Kate Johnson was born in 1962 in Manchester but has lived for sixteen years in Newport, Anglesey and Cardiff. She left work as a clerical officer to concentrate on her three young children. Her single Seren collection is called *Gods*.

Peregrine

She perches on the rim of the world,
    her nest a spattered rag-bag
    elder sticks are white longbones.

She has unpicked this rock dove,
    the wind worries at grey feathers
    pigeons racket in a cave.

She has crucified a speckled gull,
    its scared eye stares skywards
    its breast a clean bone keel.

In the teeth of a gale, spiralling
    gulls scold. Her eye is yellow fury,
    her belly is pale blown foam.

Her land is a wild quarter of
    red bracken and gorse, the peregrine
    sits hunched in a castle of rocks.

The sea sucks at the foot of the cliff.
    Far out the peregrine flies fast
    winnowing sun and cloud.

Family Grave

As my wooden casket crumbles,
my bone settles into soil.
Beneath my fleshless palms
I feel the press of someone else —
her knuckles, polished as ivory bobbins.
The petals of bone that were her face
crush beneath the lead-weight
of my skull.
My backbone folds and is caged
within those other ribs.
I am falling into the basket
of her hips.
By the movement of earthworms
I enter my mother.

Sheep

She lies inside
her own death-smell.
Even the dog ignores her.

Crows have been here
before us; they picked
the eyes out first.
    Sometimes
the dark inside
        surfaces....

They have tunnelled
into her blue drumskin
to make this vibrating cavity;
they have left nothing inside
    but a few blobs
of candlewax.

174

She must have come to die
in this place under thorns
filled with her cheesy smell
and generations of skulls.
   Nothing moves
except the ant in her nostrils
a carrion beetle
and a few flags of wool.

Crouched
   here in the dark
with her stink
and the empty goblets of her neighbours' skulls

it is hard to believe there is anything else
in the world

when outside there are larks and gorse flowers
and April's blue and bleating....

Snow

In the silence of snow
redwings are whispering
in firethorn.

An apple's orange skin
uncurls; birds peck
a flesh of crystals.

Glyn Jones

Born in Merthyr Tydfil in 1905, Glyn Jones worked as a teacher at schools in Cardiff. A noted novelist, poet, short-story writer, critic and translator, he was a fluent Welsh-speaker. His death in 1995 has inspired a renewed interest in his life and work. His well-received *Selected Poems* appeared from Seren in 1988. His *Collected Poems* and *Collected Short Stories* appeared in 1996.

Esyllt

As he climbs down our hill, my kestrel rises,
Steering in silence up from five empty fields,
A smooth sun brushed brown across his shoulders,
Floating in wide circles, his warm wings stiff.
Their shadows cut; in new soft orange hunting boots
My lover crashes through the snapping bracken.

The still, gorse-hissing hill burns, brags gold broom's
Outcropping quartz; each touched bush spills dew.
Strangely, last moment's parting was never sad,
But unreal, like my promised years; less felt
Than this intense and silver snail calligraphy
Scrawled here in the sun across these stones.

Why have I often wanted to cry out
More against his going when he has left my flesh
Only for the night? When he has gone out
Hot from my mother's kitchen, and my combs
Were on the table under the lamp, and the wind
Was banging the doors of the shed in the yard.

Watcher

At the end of the field here I have waited, and am waiting;
The eastern clouds behind the trees are soaked in blackness,
And stars come out and ripen in the clear stretches of sky.
How long shall I wait for your coming out of the waters?

The black sea beyond the field is smooth as a river,
And the red reflection of a buoy-light writhes there;
Far on the left, five fields away,
The lighted village stretches out like a glowing filament.

When shall I see you coming up golden before me,
Coming warm and full between sea and sky,
With the heavens, moon of the south, golden-green about you
When shall I see you rising warm out of the waters?

The Seagull
after Dafydd ap Gwilym

Gracing the tide-warmth, this seagull,
The snow-semblanced, moon-matcher,
The sun-shard and sea-gauntlet
Floating, the immaculate loveliness.
The feathered one, fishfed, the swift-proud,
Is buoyant, breasting the combers.
Sea-lily, fly to this anchor to me,
Perch your webs on my hand.
You nun among ripples, habited
Brilliant as paper-work, come.
Girl-glorified you shall be, pandered to,
Gaining that castle mass, her fortalice.
Scout them out, seagull, those glowing battlements,
Reconnoitre her, the Eigr-complexioned.
Repeat my pleas, my citations, go
Girlward, gull, where I ache to be chosen.
She solus, pluck up courage, accost her,
Stress your finesse to the fastidious one;

177

Use honeyed diplomacy, hinting
I cannot remain extant without her.
I worship her, every particle worships!
Look, friends, not old Merddin, hot-hearted,
Not Taliesin the bright-browed, beheld
The superior of this one in loveliness.
Cypress-shapely, but derisive beneath
Her tangled crop of copper, gull,
O, when you eye all Christendom's
Loveliest cheek — this girl will bring
Annihilation upon me, should your answer
Sound, gull, no relenting note.

Dawn Trees

Morning of cold green, grape and the golden
    Water candles, crystal in soft stars, and
The fragile bangle of a new moon's milk.

Sun lights the blue palm, rooted upon the
    Shores of her long blue pool of shadow.

Old man in mourning, his knee-bone crooked, bows
    Beneath his burden, green leaves and black wine.

Breeze stirs the olive, the great grey wrestler
    Hurls off his invisible adversary.

Now is the juniper's green breeze called joy.

The Common Path

On one side the hedge, on the other the brook:
    Each afternoon I, unnoticed, passed
The middle-aged schoolmistress, grey-haired,
    Gay, loving, who went home along the path.

That spring she walked briskly, carrying her bag
    With the long ledger, the ruler, the catkin twigs,

Two excited little girls from her class
    Chattering around their smiling teacher.

Summer returned, each day then she approached slowly,
    Alone, wholly absorbed, as though in defeat
Between water and hazels, her eyes heedless,
    Her grey face deeply cast down. Could it be
Grief at the great universal agony had begun
    To feed upon her heart — war, imbecility,
Old age, starving, children's deaths, deformities?
    I, free, white, gentile, born neither
Dwarf nor idiot, passed her by, drawing in
    The skirts of my satisfaction, on the other side.

One day, at the last instant of our passing,
    She became, suddenly, aware of me
And, as her withdrawn glance met my eyes,
    Her whole face kindled into life, I heard
From large brown eyes a blare of terror, anguished
    Supplication, her cry of doom, death, despair.
And in the warmth of that path's sunshine
    And of my small and manageable success
I felt at once repelled, affronted by her suffering,
    The naked shamelessness of that wild despair.

Troubled, I avoided the common until I heard
    Soon, very soon, the schoolmistress, not from
Any agony of remote and universal suffering
    Or unendurable grief for others, but
Private, middle-aged, rectal cancer, was dead.

What I remember, and in twenty years have
    Never expiated, is that my impatience,
That one glance of my intolerance,
    Rejected her, and so rejected all
The sufferings of wars, imprisonments,
    Deformities, starvation, idiocy, old age —
Because fortune, sunlight, meaningless success,
    Comforted an instant what must not be comforted.

Swifts

Shut-winged fish, brown as mushroom,
The sweet, hedge-hurdling swifts, zoom
Over waterfalls of wind.
I salute all those lick-finned,
Dusky-bladed air-cutters.
Could you weave words as taut, sirs,
As those swifts', great cywydd kings,
Swart basketry of swoopings?

Remembering Siani

She leaps in sunlight, her grin wicked —
With all the élan of a French forward
She brings down her blue ball,
Her silky butterscotch coat shedding
A shaken-off golden sheen, a numbness
Of yellow marigold.
    As children,
In our sunlit kitchen, we gazed down,
Enchanted, into the wonder of the newly opened
Tin of golden syrup — so are her eyes,
Golden, not treacly, darker, more amber,
Warm, firm and clear.
    The barmy Welshman who sold her,
A little thing, to us — how could he? —
Was red-haired, short-legged, bandy and long-nosed,
And so, full-grown, was she; grotesque, absurd,
But yet, beyond belief, and utterly, beautiful.
Dignified too, with a grave clown's dignity,
A comic gravity and grace
That made us want to laugh at her
And yet remain respectful, loving and enthralled.
    Never was she morose, never beat, never
Intimidated by the future, although if I
Was slow to fondle her she could pretend to pout.
We had once handsome Pompey, a dalmatian dog,

A noble creature with a dignity of stance
And grace of movement no short-arsed corgi
Ever could approach — faithful also,
And aloof and stern, but he was often sad,
(Although he died before Hiroshima),
Melancholy, poor boy, and gloomy, deeply
Cast down before the vanity of our human wishes.
   But the little corgi bitch,
Her great uncalculating charm was perpetual,
Full-time, almost professional as a geisha girl's,
But far more innocent and exuberant,
More like a dashing Russian dancer's gaiety,
Leaping uninhibited in jet-black hat of astrakhan
And dishy long green coat and buckskin cossack boots.
But she was Welsh all right, Welsh of the Welsh,
Inbred Welsh, Welsh was her first language
Although she learnt some English too,
Words like *walks,* and *lead,* and *bones* —
And when she ran in rain her coat would smell,
Not of dog, but with the pungency of Teify flannel.
   Her ancient lineage, from the era of Hywel Dda,
Predated the Welsh Herberts' and Cecils', who, like her kin,
Shot up the social ladder, becoming courtiers
High in royal trust and favour, faithful darlings
Of Elizabeths; some cousins still remain unpaid
And poor auxiliaries of Dyfed cowboys, some are seen
About that tweedy world that tramps with shooting sticks
Across the pages of the posher magazines;
Some are yet short peasants predominant in palaces.
   When our memories,
Much that we recall, more we are haunted by,
Is shameful, is of loss and tears, suffering and death —
Blessing upon the miracle of Siani, comical, even absurd,
But handsome always, faithful, loving, droll,
Who by living, being, gave poor us delight,
Who, in a morning's sunlight, would run white-bibbed
Towards us, across the glittering lawn, grinning,
Her snow-white paws scattering sunlit
Dewdrops, scattering diamonds.

Sally Roberts Jones

Born in London of Welsh parents in 1935, Sally Roberts Jones
returned to work as a librarian in Wales in the sixties. She writes
poetry and criticism and runs her own publishing house, Alun
Books, based in Port Talbot. Her single Seren volume is called
Relative Values.

'There are no trees on Anglesey'

old saying

It is not true, of course.
Slender, delicate saplings moss the Straits,
Greyhounds on leash outside their masters' chateaux;
By Penmon's well the lush growth
Droops over cress and nettle
The too-thin limbs of adolescence.
Inland the thorntrees bend
Low on the skyline, shaped by the wind:
Not beautiful these.
Wind-carved, they lean on the earth,
Grow, stubborn, from rock-banks,
Bind down the hard-purchased soil
In the stony fields.
The invisible god they house
Can't be reached by the axe.

Where Paulinus's legions
Faced druids, cat-calling hags,
The whole gamut of hell-fire,
Quiet groves flourish:

182

What Rome would destroy
The bulldozer flattens
To house new invasions.
No-one destroys the thorn trees;
They do not grow
On desirable land.
As the sculptor frees from the stone
The perfected image
So wind and water and fire
Loose the tree.
Bending, it saves itself,
Yet will not yield,
Bears beauty each year in grace notes
Of sturdy blossom.
These the inheritors:
Through the long ages
Bearing the memory
Of the falling groves.

Ellen Owen

She's a myth as much as a woman.
Grandfather's grandmother,
Remembered by name, not by place.
Ellen Owen.
Neither Mrs or Ms would express her,
What she was, what she did,
Too rigid and small for her fury.
'What she minded, she compassed' —
Is that on her grave by the Straits?
The old epitaph made for her sort?
Five husbands, a score of live children —
But nobody's brood mare.

At one moment she governed, sat prim
In her drawing-room glory of silk,
And counted the harvest of seas

Grown ripe for her pleasure.
At another, poor widow, she toiled,
Foot-weary, along the sharp stubble
For a lapful of gleanings.

And as to those husbands, who knows?
Not even their names have survived.
She endured, and they were, or were not,
Faint shadows below the grey rocks.
She was always the one in command —
Though at last, on a windy, clear day,
She too took instruction;
Walking up from the market, was told
That, a hundred years young, it was time.

For three weeks she held court.
Downstairs her daughters brewed tea,
Her respectable sons
Talked gravely of nothing, old friends
Took account of their settling day.
Then, debts answered, sins pardoned, all done,
She turned over and slept. And awoke
Elsewhere, still herself, but a saint?
Who knows? All we have are her bones.

The Glass Galleon

for my mother

That ship I brought you once,
A cobweb
Frozen in summer air,
Went down to an early wreck.
Its hull lies now, green glass,
In a deeper harbour,
Rubbed smooth with years and current:
Beside it the cherished rubble of a fleet
Grows featureless.

Pebbles across the sea-bed scour the sand
Clean of all trash;
No fever taints the shore.
Only one single rock in all that bay
Hides darkly under waves,
Is fouled with weed —
Draws, like a lodestone,
All our ships to wreck.

The Green Lady of Llŷn Fawr

She is domesticated now.
A pretty girl who spends time
Making chains from the blood-red berries.

He need not fear.
She will give, and ask nothing from him
Save a thank you or two.

So the legends decay.
No sacrifice now, the swords and the golden rings
Ripped out and preserved, on display.

Yet sometimes, in dreams,
Asleep by his golden girl,
He is troubled:

The bleating of sheep is a chant
That leads him to death; and her smile
Is the knife at his throat:
If he wakes
The red berries lie bright on his skin.

Peter Thabit Jones

Peter Thabit Jones was born in Swansea in 1951. He tutors Children's Literature for D.A.C.E., University College of Swansea, and Creative Writing for Swansea Community Education Services. His single Seren collection is *Visitors*.

Stuffed Cobra

My father sent it to me,
In a box also containing
A picture-view of Kuwait,
Broken-English letter and
A Japanese tie gay as a
Lady's silk scarf. And, poking
Steel and plucking black, I re-stitched
Its slit hood to stop the wood
Specks of pine blood trickling from it.
Then I held it, coiled to kill,
Under the cold water tap; dried
It by fire and, later,
Clear-varnished its body —
Curl of beach wood with minute eyes
And wisp of tongue — placed it on
The front window sill, to frighten
Old women and children: like
An asylum receives and
Restores a patient, then places
Him back out in the loud jungle.

Gower Delivery

For the last hot hour or more,
I have been carrying boxes
To the top step, the ninth step,
Of the front door of this exclusive,
Seaside, mock Miami Beach hotel.
Once again, up into the rancid
Back of my van; checking cold boxes
Of scampi, cod, mixed vegetables,
Plaice, hake, French fries and slabs of meat,
Against the journey-crumpled,
Delivery-note. The frozen foods
Thawing in the furnace of the van.
Once more, I struggle back up the
Crunching, gravel path. A woman
Guest, as desirable as an iced lager,
Smiles from a high, sun-demanding balcony.
Two bold children, their ice-cream cones dripping
In the mischievous heat, hurry
Down the quaking path to the crowded
Beach: the dead sky shrouds sea and sand.
Back to my sea-blue van — with the painted,
Smiling fish and short-haired, apple-cheeked
Butchers on its doors. The sun has gone mad!
I guzzle the last sour drops
Of lukewarm Coca Cola in my can,
Wipe my wet brow in my shirt-sleeves
And stoop down to re-tie a limp shoelace.
Glancing up at the balcony,
I find my golden Eve has gone.
Then the front door opens and she comes out,
Her tanned body testing her bikini's strength.
Smiling, she moves to the car park
And gets into a dark red sportscar.
I return to the burning hotel,
For a man's unruly signature.

187

Tim Liardet

Tim Liardet was born in London in 1949, graduated from the University of York and currently lives in Shropshire. Having worked in marketing and information technology he is now a freelance writer. His poetry has been published extensively on both sides of the Atlantic and his recent second Seren collection, is titled *Fellini Beach*.

Summer Storm

1.
The pressure quadruples. Insects beneath it
Crawl under each leaf. The guttering's spider
Wobbles its rigging. Old and immense
The sycamores gather — all stillness and resignation —
The shallows of their gloom upon which
The Toby Jugs squander a puffed glance
Creep indoors. No lights. The dark garden's
Abandoned mowing maroons its ragged island
As the clock beats strong, against the Approach.

The fields are sensuous, rank with odours.
Out of the distance — suddenly overhead —
The firmamental boulders are being
Tipped, disgruntled, grumbling round.
One electrical suture splices down.
The first hesitant drops plip on the glass
Like the moths, their inearthly eye-lights
Blundering against a curtailed obstruction.
One ungainly duck flaps panicking up
Across the gloom caught in sudden daylight.
The trough bubbles. Each leaf begins to bounce.

2.
My tongue found your wetness at last.
Spread wide, breasts lapsing back, eyes shut
And head to one side — hair spread on a surface
As if on water, as if perfectly weightless —
You lay above, warm feathers settling round you.
All lights gone, whatever remained of the storm
Moved around us and the open-curtained room
In which we moved together almost eerily
By its eerie light, your feet in the air
And toes straining up, to fetch our noises
From their submerged-places through our scorched throats.
The broken-hedged fields of flattened hay
Out under the sycamores flashed in the last
Innocuous spasms, framed by the window,
Shadowing the tensed vertebrae along my spine.
Belly to belly, moisture into moisture.

Under Upper Tier

To avoid the glazed queues at Tea
I trouble the row between overs,
To assuage fermenting discomfort,
The gaseous contents of the can...
Cracked tiles, shall we say, map relief.

A gloom behind the sunlit field.
As sudden as the jets that flush
Away, in the stand above, the roar
Of ruptured concentration, a span
Underneath clattering with fresh claps.

And I know that someone (walking back
Feeling perhaps the ghost of the ghost
Of the dead thud on the pad) is out.
His mood, checked for cameras, matches
My single overwhelmed expletive.

He walks from sunlight to the gloom.
I walk from the gloom to sunlight.
A ball blurred. Above me consensus
Gathers like the amplified sound
Of rainfall. Grass warms. Cisterns hiss.

Palimpsest for a Radio Play

Wetherton polishes the Captain's forty spoons.
He replaces them in velvet casts like snug instruments.

He lays out the crumpled dog-rose in *The Oxford English*
And bemoans the Daimler's savage lace-work of rust.

Baggage without handles! Without help Wetherton
Must keep the pains and visions from the older man's head

Like the voracious rats from the strawberry nets
Or bluebottles from kidneys staining the scrubbed table.

He has led the Captain back, confused and pathological,
Muttering bastardized verse with mud up to his knees;

He has heard his piss clattering on the foliage
Of the crepuscular alders, making his voice strange:

Cover her face, she died young; perfection is far away.
I shall sleep all night in my leaking galoshes.

The dusty-glassed lodge house, twenty years from India,
Swims in the chiaroscuro of its sycamore:

Their dependence externalises in a shabby order;
They bear each other's muted contusions with

An oblique if sacrosanct refusal to comment at all.
The magazines fade on the sill with the dead flies;

The broken ball-cock has been broken for a year;
It is the order of the lawn before the moles push up.

Into the other side of the lodge (it bestrides the Gate)
Two spinsters assumed to be sisters move suddenly in:

Efficient in unpacking, alike, they sustain an air
Of determined insouciance, swinging their cello-cases.

The glow of an alien taste illumines isolation:
The small hours lap the little weights in their hems.

Wetherton sees one night the newly hung curtain draw back
And a pale blur of flesh dip at the steamy glass.

He fancies that he sees one patient sister yielding to
The other's comb, and hearing drifts of a soft adagio,

Peeps to see the two of them sitting naked with
Their cellos between their knees, their unravelled hair

Falling where they stoop to the sawing of their bows,
Long fingers active on the elongated strings.

Through a gin-obtuseness and the Captain's ear-hair
The image is conveyed, still cold from the night air....

Invited to tea, the women say little, exchanging looks,
Treated with the same degree of stilted attention

As were the barley field's shocked copulating couple
To whom the Captain raised his hat, as they covered up.

A corridor of trunks, discardments — no man's land —
Links the two men to the two women over the Gate.

In the camera obscura their movements are monitored.
Wetherton begins to relish, too much for self-esteem,

191

The weekly execution of the remonstrating hen
In an explosion of feathers. The strike from nowhere —

A storm over gravid wheat, breaking in the mind —
Leaves his right hand as useless as the latest hen's:

This coincides with the sudden moving out of the women.
The deep vibrato of tensed strings at twilight

Is replaced by the usual background of estate crows.
It is as if, so to speak, the women were never there.

The Captain brings some warm eggs to the wheelchair
And lifts the little cosies: *voilà*, and taps spoon on shell.

And on a summer evening of deepening silences
That enter the upper room with the scent of mown hay

He unfolds the cloth and painstakingly identifies
The specimens, pinned out and helpless, under the glass.

After forty years of squeaking the glass Wetherton
Perceives the pins. He begins to wear the Captain's

Admittedly tatty and oversized plimsolls. His voice changes:
Cover her face, cover her face, cover her face.

Fellini Beach

The two in costume pursued across the dune
Are held in focus all along a temporary track
By men who ride a camera all afternoon.

The booms scuttle, bit-players endure, immune
By now to the squealy megaphones calling back
The two in costume pursued across the dune.

And everyone's too hot, to repeat so soon
The umpteenth identical take, led out of the black
By men who ride a camera all afternoon.

When the signal's given, the gaffers importune.
A regatta of parasols surges, as if to attack
The two in costume pursued across the dune.

The blank-faced locals — desultory and jejune —
To and fro in the heat, shown only bum and back
By men who ride a camera all afternoon.

The crowd loops forward, in a demilune;
All watch the hugely fat, through each blown yashmak:
The two in costume pursued across the dune
By men who ride a camera all afternoon.

Hart Crane on *The Orizaba*

Drowned in The Gulf of Mexico, April, 1932

Pennies for porpoises that bank the keel.
The declamatory waters at the stern reel
And divide, three hundred hazy miles north
Of Havana, sad engines trembling forth
Toward the steamy shambles of Manhattan.
Assuaging humours lost and largely misbegotten
The waves at noon, in their hissing rapture,
Slap the ship's metal. This is an end.
There is no arrival, and no departure
To be had. *Break off — descend, descend.*
Dive, thoughts, down, and say I sent thee hence.
The ship's rail is the last of difference.
Take me, then, take me, thou convulsive foam,
Expunge my voice and silence in thine own
With dismissal or welcome, beyond all harm
Dilute me in thy wide immensity of calm.
Down, down, down, let surrender be complete,
My arms thrown out wide, as if in flight.

Sea will use the eyelets of my boyish boots
To spurt the first chamber, compressing my suit's
Blown stitching of trapped air from which a green
Ink will escape like the blood from a vein.
Air and water, in hard lumps, forcing through
My wide dissolving mouth and hands will break into
The sanctum of my lungs and swelling underwear
Like a massage of bubbles, until my hair
Dawdles in slow calm and from my ticking watch
I shall be parted finally, a fumbled catch
Of otiose gold, spun slowly down, to lose
Its last pretension like a dead man's shoes
Creating some disturbance in the silt.
Turbines at the microphones — everything spilt;
A man who tumbled, one arm round his neck,
Through striped fathoms from the sunlit deck
(Upon which the weight of my overcoat will
Collapse in its folds, stuffed, buckle-flung, still
A sad and half-occupied comfort, as if
Squandering a gesture against the final rift).
Above it, esurient gulls, that wheel and turn
Shrieking of hunger. Who will there be to learn
How badly, if at all, the thrown world sleeps?
This fabulous shadow only the sea keeps.

Hilary Llewellyn-Williams

Born in 1952 in Kent, Hilary Llewellyn-Williams has made her home in west Wales for some years, most recently near Llanelli. She has also travelled in Europe and North America. Her most recent Seren collection is titled *Book of Shadows* and contains an ambitious sequence based on the life and work of the Renaissance philosopher, monk and poet, Giordano Bruno.

Feeding the Bat

At first it was a small cold palmful
a hunched and sorry scrap, clenched still
but for an infinitesimal buzz and tremble

as we passed it from hand to hand
half fearful that the buzzing might explode
into uncontrollable flight. So we found

a box, and a place by the stove, and scrounged
a spoonful of dogfood from the corner shop
and waited. When the scratching started

we crowded round to listen: it was alive!
Lifting it out, it seemed larger; it moved
its clever head from side to side, gave

delicate soundings. Two eyes, dark points of light
gleamed, not at all blind, and long questioning
fingers gripped mine. Whiskered like a cat

with a cat's silken cunning it consented
to be fed from the end of a stick, opened
a triangle mouth wide, and dipped and lunged

manoeuvering meatlumps in. Laughing, we squeezed
waterdrops onto its nose, to hear it sneeze
minute bat-sneezes, to watch the supple greedy

slip of a tongue flick the droplets down.
As it warmed, it got bolder, nipping our skin
with needle teeth, unfolding its tucked wings

turning its goblin face to the window, where
milky chilled spring daylight lured
it to sudden flight, skimming at head height

a strange slow flutter, followed by a whisper
of displaced air. Awaiting a change of weather
we hung it in a bag to sleep over the stairs

and roused it for feeding. After the second day
it arched its back to be stroked, and played
a biting game, neck stretched impossibly

backwards, slyly grinning. That evening, the sun
shone. We carried it in its bag to a vacant barn
by the river. It squealed as I left it there, long

angry squeals; but I was firm. I would not
be quite a witch yet, stroking and feeding a bat
my ears tuned to its music, swooping, flitting about —

though I lean out to the buoyant dusk, for all that.

from *The Tree Calendar*
Holly

July 8–August 4

Here in high summer, holly sets fruit
that will redden come Christmas.
Its prickles gloss and crackle in the sun.
Those deathless leaves make holly king.

This tree is holy, but not kind. What
is this holiness? What gift of grace
is so sharp-edged, dark-branched, hedged
with superstition, crowned with thorn?

Last summer's holly scratched my small
son as he climbed a bank, from rib
to breastbone a long stripe, with beads
of berry-blood, a flaxen Christ, arms up

and crying. This summer's rain
has blighted our best crops; but the trees
thrive, the trees take precedence. Green
under grey skies: reign of wood and water.

As the days shorten, holly's power grows:
ripening power, the birth power, power
from behind the eyes, dream power, spear-
leaved and bitter-barked and full of berries.

Holly saplings under graveyard yews
like prongs of resurrection, spring
from the shadows. The yews red-fleshed
and folded secretly, gave birth to them.

Blood mixed with soil was the old way
harvests grew fat, and holly ruled the feast.
My torn child heals: a ragged silver line
across his breast, fades as he flourishes.

197

Breadmaking

Forgive the flour under my fingernails
the dabs of dough clinging to my skin:
I have been busy, breadmaking.
So easy, the flakes falling feathery
into the warm bowl, as I dip and measure
and pour the foaming treasured brown
yeast down to the ground wheat grain.
O as the barm breaks and scatters
under my working fingers like a scum
of tides on shifting sands, the secret cells
swell, you can smell their life
feeding and beating like blood
in my bunched palms
while I lift the lump and slap it back again.

It moves, like a morning mushroom,
a breathing side, stirring, uncurling
animal nudged from sleep; so I pummel
and thump and knuckle it into shape
to see it unwind like a spring
soft as a boneless baby on the table.
I have covered it now: let it grow
quietly, save for the least rustle
of multiplication in the damp bundle
telling of motion in the fattening seeds.
Its body's an uproar as I open the burning door —
it gives one final heave, and it blossoms out
to the brown loaf I have spread for you.
Taste the butter touching its heart like snow.

The Trespasser

My fingers are sweet with stealing
blackcurrants. Among tall weeds
ropes of them, thick and ripe like secrets.
I move in shadow, sharp-eyed, listening.

A distant car sets my spine quivering.
Bold as a bird I pull the berries down,
gather them in. Their smell excites me.

The house is blind: no-one is living here,
yet I am trespassing. Each summer the owners
come for a week or two, cut grass,
clean windows, stare out from their gate.
But the river sings all year; and swifts make
nests, flowers bloom and fruit
ripens, and snow sweeps the lawn
smooth for the prints of foxes.

In spring there were daffodils, massed gold
and white narcissi; I ran in the rain
to gather armfuls, carrying them home
to shine in my windows. I live by here
every day, in poverty. What the hedges grow,
what's in the hills, I take back for my children.

Great polished blackcurrants in my fist.
They drop in the bag, grow fat.
Tonight I'll mix them with sugar, and steam
them slowly. The dark, sour, smoky taste;
my children's red mouths and chins,
their high, bird voices. Each year the trees
step forward round the house: I notice that.
In the autumn, I'll come for apples.

Brynberllan

This is a place where nothing really grows
but water: water and stones.

And concrete bungalows, and lost holdings.

Tilt of water from the mountainside
pushes under the road, and stones grow
overnight in our gardens: rainbuffed hard

perennials. We're on the flank
of the wind, even in summer.

But years ago, this was an apple orchard.

Rows and patterns of trees, all the way
down to the stream called *Comely;*
mossy barked, their dark blue stems at dusk,
the sun spread white at dawn on slopes
of blossom; warm air, stirred thick
with honey. Humming and swarms, and then
the smell of ripe fruit: those small
sharp western apples.

Crowded faces, bushels and basketfuls.

Everyone there, at work in the branches,
measuring the loads, brown-armed
and busy. Shouts in the crisp leaves.
Children rolling windfalls down the hill.
Foxes nosing at night through bruised grass.

And apple smoking in the soul-fires.

I think the traffic worsens year by year
just passing through. Rain's harsher too:
laced with acid and caesium, it fills
the stream called *Comely* and the stream
called *Blossom*. Nothing flourishes.

Yet sometimes we'll distill, between breath

and breath, a taste of sweetness:
yes, even now, a rustling of leaves
a blossom-drift. Between low flakes
of October sunlight, treeshapes flicker;
and evenings to the West bring cloud-landscapes
rising like a range of wooded hills,
a place of apple-orchards. Not here: beyond
reach, elsewhere, forsaken, forfeited.

The Sealwife

One day I shall find my skin again:
my own salt skin, folded dark, its fishweed stink
and tang, its thick warm fat, great thrusting tail

all mine: and I'll take it and shake it out
to the wind, draw it over me cool and snug,
laugh softly, and slip back to my element.

I shall find my stolen skin, hidden by you
for love (you said) that night the sea-people danced,
stashed in some cleft in the rocks where I may not go

but used to go, and dance too, stepping free
in my new peeled body, the stalks of my legs in the moon-
light strange, my long arms shaping the sky

that have narrowed their circles down
to the tasks of these forked hands: lifting,
fetching, stirring, scrubbing, embracing — the small

stiff landlocked movements. In the sea
I plunged and swam for my own joy, sleek and oiled,
and I loved at will in rolling-belly tides.

Here love is trapped between the walls of a house
and in your voice and eyes, our children's cries;
whose boundaries I've understood, a language

learnt slowly, word by word. You've been dear and good —
how you would sing to me, those wild nights!
— and oil my breasts by firelight, and dip down

to taste my sea-fluids. I'd forget to mourn
those others then, trawling the flickering deeps.
Now I cry for no reason, and dream of seals:

an ocean booms in the far cave of my ear
and voices tug at me as I stand here
at the window, listening. Our children sleep

201

and by daylight they run from me. Their legs
strong, their backs straight, bodies at ease
on solid ground — though they play for hours on the shore

between sand and sea, and scramble the wet rocks
gladly. It won't be long now, the waiting:
they love to poke and forage in the cracks

of the cliffs; sharpeyed, calling, waving.

Andarax

Almería, Andalusia

On the map, a broad blue sinuous line said
water. Dark, fluid and cool
from the snows of Sierra Nevada,
bordered by orange groves and thirsty vines
threading and falling, a ripple between banks

because in Wales a river means moving water
I pictured that. So nothing prepared me for
nothing — that yawning ditch of dust,
that void, that absence. Sun spat
and crackled in the stones. Baked mud

cracked open. A long bridge spanned
the gulf. Everything the bleached-out dun
of old shit. On a ruinous site nearby
a JCB dug slowly: the dust went ten feet down —
further, the whole way. Crossing the no-river,

crossing the Andarax, I shuddered; my throat
dry as a lizard's, my eyes peeled raw.
Down to bedrock. Even its name's a cough,
a rasp, a drought. It does not summon liquid,
shadowy pools, slack shallows, slide of fish.

It's the name of a slaughtered dragon;
a mythical beast; a fossil; a chained Book
of Spells, with dark parchment pages: *Andarax.*
Somebody mentioned a winter legend of water,
snow-floods. I could not believe it:

that was too long ago, in another country.

Christopher Meredith

Born in Tredegar in 1954, Christopher Meredith lives in Powys with his family. A noted novelist (*Shifts, Griffri*), his most recent Seren collection of poetry is *Snaring Heaven*. He currently divides his time between writing and lecturing in the writing programme at the University of Glamorgan.

Desk

I rescued you, splinted your broken legs.
Forty years or so had scummed you dark
With ink, dead skin, the rain of dust, the grease
Of knees and cuffs and fingertips, with work

Done routinely by the bored but paid.
I unlidded you, cut wedges, made true
The skewed split joints, machined human gluten
Off the boards. My carpentry of nails and glue

Fell short of craft but was informed by love.
I plugged you, cleaned your handles, planed,
Saw purity of copper and the packed white grain.
Some wounds were healed, the depth of others learned

— No restoration ever is complete.
People at work, the children and the staff,
Gave you their own disfigurement —
Not inborn malice but the hurt of graft

That rubbed a hole in their humanity.
And I played Samaritan out of guilt
Of sorts. Worked out, I was looking for my
Small re-creation as you were rebuilt.

Relidded, drawers eased, your eight legs firm,
Beeswax bringing alive the fans and bars
Of tan and yellow grain, you are a place
For another sort of work. We're both scarred

But the worm in each of us is dead.
I'm not paid much, but neither am I bored
Nor hurt by work's attrition as we go
To real work. This page, the silence, these words.

In Ebenezer Churchyard, Sirhowy

On this grey smear of a weak day
the rasp of a forced gate
explodes impossibly.
Rubbish cast by the wall
blares in the eyes.
In winter light, you think,
it should all break and fade.
Drizzle smudges all the edges
makes eyes thirst for colour
soaks without sensation
makes feet soundless
the air sodden bland and comfortless.
In the grey nothing edges of graves
butt pallidly into vision, geometry
scraped on the rain.

There is no tradition to say this.
Here is no stone tower to crutch
a wrong church nor yew to undermine
with his older root the shallow ruler. Only
a shanty-town of leaning slabs
picked over with a fuss of letters
curled to remember the sweep of a nib.
There quench the eye.
Jane Pryce diweddar o Swydd Feirionydd
dead with her baby and others respectable

205

only their trades in English
all quietly rubbing to nothing on the air.

The children from the flats
have gone home on their bikes
taken the colour with them
except by the wall on the beaten grass
the busted plastic bag leaks cellophane
and printed cardboard darkening with wet
but clear enough for eyes to seize
to drink from greedily
in a bare place in the rain blur.

So these are the ones who walked from the west.
Twelve shillings a week instead of eight.
Cadernid ffydd.
See the upshot:
rain that runs on the smashed stones
a drinker from a broken cup.

Sheep

This one, you guess, looking at me, is the leader.
His stare is not a challenge. Nothing. Just a stare.
And the way the others clutter behind him in the wagon.
This, you think, is some photo of an old war. Clothes
ragged, cropped heads, children dazed calling for food,
all the thin legs merded with crammed travel
and eyes indifferent with many deaths.
The eyes, you think, must haunt the guards at the compound gate
hinting of seeing through all things.
Perhaps you feel yourself melt a little, feel naked
when I look at you.

We have been a rich vein for you,
for your languages and rites.
Your god was one of us, you say
yet also our crooked captor, caring for us
clinical with our surgery

his outstretched manpicture your mangod picture.
We have been: The Lost, The Wanderers, The Sufferers.
You have set us on high and taken our flesh.
This is no injustice. Only irony.

Sitting with your car door pushed open in the afternoon
one foot on the earth
tea in the flask, a map in the glovebox
you can look around the country where we are kept
and feel no wryness —
feel warmed even, in the dozing lanes
hate the smoke and motorways you came out of
before you turn back.
But you catch my eye a moment on the passing wagon.
Reflected there you see all the rolling vale
your fallen eden unfolded and become
a heaving green belsen.

Segovia on Record

Fingers trap the moments on the frets
and weave them into coats of sound —
the right hand's hard and glassy at the bridge
or at the soundhole fluting,
the left strokes lovely ramirez's neck,
jigsaws fretted screens at the alhambra,
holds the coat up to be seen

and so

no fingers catch the moments on the frets —
the imageless precision of the coat
masks the weaver's hands; no screen, no thought, no
self, no coat — only limitless technique
worked on a sounding abacus, and always
the black disc spiralling towards its end,
the hiss of time like rain on the roof.

Kathy Miles

Kathy Miles was born in 1952 in Liverpool, though she has lived for some years now in west Wales, where she currently works as a librarian at the Univerity of Wales, Lampeter. She has recently edited a Gomer anthology of poetry called *The Third Day: Landscape and the Word*. Her Seren collection is *The Rocking-Stone*.

The Knitter

Grey wool on white-bone needles,
growing a place for toes and fingers
to hide their winter cold in.
Her feet on the warmstone fireplace
tap to the grating rhythm.
A clicking, like several clocks gone mad
from boredom of a single note.
Knit one, purl one, slip stitch over.
A cable might snake out painfully,
or a moss that creeps across the floor,
a soft grey fungus.
Strands like tangled hair caught in barbed wire.
Sometimes the flames confuse her eyes
with chaos as she passes over rows
and knots unravel, just at the moment of turning.
Sweaters and mittens fall from her swollen fingers,
socks and cardigans, all in a different mode.
They, out in the fields or flushed in the pubs,
talk proudly of the cosy figure
made larger by the fire's thrown shadow.

Strong and sharp and slippery are the needles,
pushing through the greasy wool with ease.
Only in her hands are the grey threads strangled,
hard and fast, to a pattern of intricate weaving.

Dragons

Believing that dragons were dead
(old legends take the longest time to die)
and still in our country-childhood,
it seemed those moulded, wrinkled spines
were natural to a hill,
and even when it turned a little, sighing,
shedding its lizard-green and feudal browns,
we only saw the mark of seasons passing.
And when the mist lay, lazy as a lover,
covering the limbs of the river,
stretching and moaning thinly in his sleep,
it was, in innocence, no more than early dew.
(No dragons' breath can compromise
the hard relief of fairy tales.)

But first was the proof of his footprints,
clawed in raised lines, like wounds across
the field. And then, one night, a hint
of distant fire betrayed a scarlet trail
of secret paths along the fading sky-line.
Now, like all the rest, we are his slaves.
His skin is harsh on our hands in the
morning: bringing blood springing
to the finger-tips, scraping the frosted
ashes in the hearth. His language
is raw — old words, that roar strange
alphabets. We dare not disobey.

Woman of Flowers (Blodeuwedd)

She is not made of meadowsweet,
conjured from broom and oak.

Her flowers are the jealous green stems
of roses, dark as poison-bottles,
bitter as taste of bark.

She drowns in nightshade
with its evening dreams of violence,
ivy's deadly sweetness.

Owl-change hunts her in
its monthly kill. She longs
to be flowers again, petal-scented,
falling to the strongness of a man.
Now she has birds' wisdom,
sweeps across dark landscapes,
she is predator, wants death;
claws sharpen in the evening holocaust.

Robert Minhinnick

Born in Neath in 1952, Robert Minhinnick lives in south Wales where he is a noted environmental activist, essayist, editor, critic and poet. Author of six volumes of poetry, his recent Seren collection, *Hey Fatman*, chronicles trips to Brazil and America. His book of essays, *Watching the Fire Eater*, was Welsh Book of the Year, 1993.

Driving in Fog

Driving in fog I part the crowded air,
Then the night falls huge and white across the car.

It is as if I stopped believing in the world
The dark conceals, preferring the immense, cold

Flowerings of fog the headlights stain
To dull amber, the solderings of rain

That glisten on the crawling vehicle.
Yet I never seem to break its streaming wall,

Never reach that moment I can rightly say
Here it begins: always it remains a yard away

In the blurred crowding of fields that overhang
The road, the pale entangling yarns

Of my own breath. Here is not the rain's
Assault, the sullen-strange communion

Of the snow. This is no weather but the bland
Present's arrest, for even the trees stand

Like inked letters half-erased. All traffic
Stops. The fog's white sweat gives radiance to the dark.

In a shrunken world I wait for it to pass,
But the fog like countless faces crowds the glass.

Rhys

Best of all I see him in the evening,
The stock of a shotgun cooling behind
A coat, woodpigeon's down plastered
Over his shirtfront. A guilty look,
But laughter under a shock of glossy curls:
Rhys, a squat Mediterranean type
Who kept his dirty tan all winter long.

We watched him over the kitchen table,
His son and I, as he broke down
A carburettor, the black grease oozing
From the opened valves, pieces of wrecked
Motorbike spread over the yard.
He talked of the job in the tinplate works
And the way the glowing metal sheets,

Incandescent as lava, came rolling
Towards him, the taste of his own sweat
In his mouth. That was the living
They gave him. Much better the one
He made himself, tuning the huge
Coughing Triumphs to full-throttled song,
Spinning them round in deafening

Rodeos over the mountainside,
Or setting out on evening expeditions,
Bringing us with him in a race downhill,

212

Glimpsing the moths he dashed from the grass,
Rising like sparks and vanishing,
Running headlong down to the invisible
Ffornwg, its high current moving east

And away, a crown of foam winking
Like beer-froth. And then he'd slip aside,
Deft hands and a murderous purpose
Opening the wire around private land,
And I would wait, thinking of the pigeon
Plucked and headless, the rusted bones
Of metal that he wrenched from the machine.

On the Llŷn Fawr Hoard in the National Museum of Wales

The fish slide through the lake's cool grip
As the buttresses of Craig y Llŷn
Throw shadows on the water,
The orange quilts of spruce dust underfoot.
Piece by piece the hoard is recovered:
Iron black and twisted as fernroots,
Cauldrons spilling their memorials
To ancient sunlight, millennia of seeds,
The pollen of two thousand buried springs
Emerging from the dark throat of Llŷn Fawr.

Redeemed from that cold lakewater
They lie in white electric pools;
This spearhead's mottling leaf colour,
Its shaft missing, lake-eaten,
Sickles like the beaks of swans
Worked in inextinguishable
Bronze light, a sword's metal
Burned charcoal-black, the pattern
Of erosion delicate as lace.

Presented here no small sophistication
Of the metalworker's art, that art's

213

Acknowledgement of something greater than itself —
The cauldron's firm belly of bronze
Yellow as roof-moss, triumphant sphere,
The pin-bolts, brooches, weaponry
Offered to the waters of the lake
In sure sacrifice, their molten substance
Pouring outside the cold cast of time.

Yet saved, they are safe, as remarkable
Only as the tools of my own household.
Behind the glass they are as young as I,
The glass that returns my own scrutiny.
History is not this gear of bronze,
Its patina teal-green;
Rather, it is how it was used,
The association of metal and mind.

Eelers

Around the wrecks the congers weave
Their convoluted shapes through decks and cabins,
The sea-invaded rooms of unmarked ships.

Oozing, mottled like orchids,
They are appetite in a sheath of muscle,
Ragged as sleeves pulled inside out.

So ceaseless eels haunt colliers and smacks,
The silt-encrusted cargoes of the sea bottom
Until they take the barb, the reel's arrow.

Then each gill is a flower, a pulse amongst
The wounds. Jack-knives and lump-hammers
The eelers' armoury, gaffs and shovels

Rise against the instinct of their rage.
And the mouths of eels twist like the mouths of dogs,
Their bodies are branches, bits of hose

Beneath the oilskin of the conger fishermen.
I've seen these crowd the greasy flags
Of harbours when a motor-launch comes in:

Men high-booted, zipped against the wind,
Their catch preserved in melting ice — mackerels'
Blue tortoiseshell like fishermens' tattoos

A sudden drift of bodies over the dock,
And the congers hung on chains, ferociously torn,
Their mouths agape like beaten, senile men.

Big Pit, Blaenafon

Coalfaces dividing like a star.
Our eyes' quick sweep to left and right
As down some supermarket aisle.

Under the rock a museum of work
And death; their illusions of dignity.
We see what we should never have believed.

And forbidden, out of bounds, the other shafts
Sealed off with their gas and broken track,
The fossil-gleam, in darkness, of our history.

The Looters

The helicopter cameras
Bring us the freeze frames.
A black sea outlines each peninsula
As snow finer than marble dust
Blurs the steeples of the spruce.
Bad weather, the wisdom goes
Brings a community together.
Tonight the screen is a mirror
And the news is us.

At a house in Bedlinog
A drift has left its stain
Like a river in flood
Against the highest eaves.
There will be a plaque placed there soon
As if for some famous son,
While the cataract at Cwm Nash
Is a thirty foot long stalactite
Full of eyes and mouths
And the dazzling short circuits
Of a pillar of mercury.
An icicle uncirclable by three men.

Abandoned on the motorway
The container lorries are dislocated
Vertebrae. The freeze has broken
The back of our commerce
While on the farms, the snow-sieged
Estates, people return
To old technologies.

Meat is hung in double rows,
The carcasses identified
By the slashing beams.
Each one looms hugely,
Puzzling as a chrysalis
Under its silver condom of frost.
They sway like garments on a rack
When padlocks break and the freezer-
Doors swing out. It is too cold
Here to trail blood, where bread
Is frozen into breeze-blocks
And ten thousand tubes of lager
Sparkle under their ripping caul.
As flashlights zigzag up the wall
Tights turn red and tropical bronze
In each thin wallet.

The stranded drivers sleep in schools,
Their groups determined to uphold
The constitution of the snow.
Families smile through thermos-steam,
A child with her kitten, blue
As a cinder, sucking a blanket:
The usual cast of winter's news
As the commentary runs its snowplough
Through the annihilating white.

Outside, the cars are scoops
Of cumulus, and toboggans
Polish gutters in the drifts.
We never see the looters.
They move somewhere in the darkness
Through the blizzard, beyond the thin
Bright crescent of the screen,
Those people who have understood the weather
And make tomorrow's news.

World War II comes to XXI Heol Eglwys

Even without a blackout
There was not much to show.
A street of cottages and whitewashed pub
Well used to the art of dousing
    Every trace of light.

You knew the Heinkel's unique drone —
Big, angry maybug trapped in a shade —
Yet here was one lower, and faltering.

The Swansea bombs were a murmur at dusk
But this was the first you had ever heard fall:
    Thin steam from a kettle;
    The whine of sap in a sycamore;
    Mosquito's itchy piccolo.

217

Under the table you felt the house's gentle shift,
Making itself more comfortable.
A joist shuddered, perhaps a slate
Escaped its nail.

And the next morning
Stood out in the field staring into the crater
That 500 pounds of German dynamite had dug.

At the rim you found a cow's horn
Polished like the haft of a walking-stick,
And noted the mattresses of roots, silver now,
In the wall of the pit.

'If the buggers could aim', your mother had said,
Shaking the plaster out of the tablecloth,
'They'd be dangerous'.

Hey Fatman

Me? I was only watching. Nothing else.
It had been one hundred degrees that day
And I'm not used to frying. So I took a seat
Outside and ordered a drink.
The beer came in a glass like a test-tube,
The colour of that monkey, the golden one,
They're trying to save around there,
The one with the mane like a lion.
And Christ, it tasted cold as a dentist's drill.

But after a while I felt the energy
To look around. And I saw
What I expected to see from a street like that:
The last soccer players on the beach,
A big surf pounding, angry, futile
In a place where it always stopped its charge,
And a beggar eating fire,
Walking up and down outside the restaurants,
A magician folding banknotes for his pimp.

At the bar stood the boss in a mildewed tux,
The sweat hanging off him in icicles.
He looked at me once and passed over —
Not important, not a player tonight.
I ordered another to make him doubt,
But he never blinked. You can't buy style.
So I studied his empire's neon sign
Out on the pavement. There was a moth on it
With wings like two South Americas.

It was bigger than my hand. But either
Nobody had seen it or nobody cared.
I wanted to scare it off that scorching globe,
Grab its wings like the old man's black lapels,
But it was impossible to move.
I couldn't get out of my chair,
Couldn't speak. So I sat and looked,
With a radioactive thirst, at the bar
And its imperceptible protocols.

The women were in by now, four of them
At the counter, each holding a drink
With an hibiscus flower in it, and a straw:
One white, one black, two mulatto,
Like my beer. In ones and twos they'd get up
And stroll outside to the pavement,
Amongst the tables, sometimes out of sight,
Wandering around the expense accounts,
As the city's electricity came on.

They weren't collecting for charity,
That's for certain. I couldn't understand
A word, but I knew what their smiles said
As they squeezed past, what their fingernails
Meant as they chimed against glass,
The stick-on ones, red as foxgloves:
Hey fatman, that's what they said;
Almost without saying it, if you know what I mean.
Because that's all it takes in a place like that.

219

Their earrings said it, their crossed
And uncrossed legs: and off they'd go
With the turks in singlets,
The executives in their button-downs,
Up a darkened stair behind the bar,
And the old man there in opera black
Would smile with his blue iguana lips
As he held the door for them, then pulled it fast,
His armpits dimpled like a garlic-press.

Ten minutes later you'd think there were four
Different girls. Not so. The younger ones
Were older now, the brunettes reborn as blondes.
And they'd suck their drinks and circulate,
Trailing a perfume through the room
Of their own sweat, like a herb crushed underfoot.
Hey fatman, it said to the night,
To the brass propellers of the fan
That uttered ceaselessly its quiet scream.

I watched the moth float down like charred paper.
Over the walls the baby roaches ran
Warning of fire, waving their brown arms.
Down through the haloes in my glass
I saw a furnace glow, the table blistering.
A man in the mirror tried to douse his boiling eyes,
But the women of the city combed their hair,
Buckled on silver, strapped on gold,
Then stepped once more out on to its hot coals.

Leslie Norris

Born in Merthyr Tydfil in 1921, Leslie Norris is the author of eleven collections of poetry as well as published short stories. He has lived for some years in the U.S. where he is Humanities Professor of Creative Writing at Brigham Young University, Utah. His last collection of poetry was *A Sea in the Desert*. His *Collected Poems* and *Collected Stories* appeared in 1996.

The Ballad of Billy Rose

Outside Bristol Rovers Football Ground —
The date has gone from me, but not the day,
Nor how the dissenting flags in stiff array
Struck bravely out against the sky's grey round —

Near the Car Park then, past Austin and Ford,
Lagonda, Bentley, and a colourful patch
Of country coaches come in for the match
Was where I walked, having travelled the road

From Fishponds to watch Portsmouth in the Cup.
The Third Round, I believe. And I was filled
With the old excitement which had thrilled
Me so completely when, while growing up,

I went on Saturdays to match or fight.
Not only me; for thousands of us there
Strode forward eagerly, each man aware
Of tingling memory, anticipating delight.

We all marched forward, all except one man.
I saw him because he was paradoxically still,
A stone against the flood, face upright against us all,
Head bare, hoarse voice aloft, blind as a stone.

I knew him at once, despite his pathetic clothes;
Something in his stance, or his sturdy frame
Perhaps, I could even remember his name
Before I saw it on his blind-man's tray. Billy Rose.

And twenty forgetful years fell away at the sight.
Bare-kneed, dismayed, memory fled to the hub
Of Saturday violence, with friends to the Labour Club,
Watching the boxing on a sawdust summer night.

The boys' enclosure close to the shabby ring
Was where we stood, clenched in a resin world,
Spoke in cool voices, lounged, were artificially bored
During minor bouts. We paid threepence to go in.

Billy Rose fought there. He was top of the bill.
So brisk a fighter, so gallant, so precise!
Trim as a tree he stood for the ceremonies,
Then turned to meet George Morgan of Tirphil.

He had no chance. Courage was not enough,
Nor tight defence. Donald Davies was sick
And we threatened his cowardice with an embarrassed kick.
Ripped across both his eyes was Rose, but we were tough

And clapped him as they wrapped his blindness up
In busy towels, applauded the wave
He gave his executioners, cheered the brave
Blind man as he cleared with a jaunty hop

The top rope. I had forgotten that day
As if it were dead for ever, yet now I saw
The flowers of punched blood on the ring floor,
As bright as his name, I do not know

How long I stood with ghosts of the wild fists
And the cries of shaken boys long dead around me,
For struck to act at last, in terror and pity
I threw some frantic money, three treacherous pence —

And I cry at the memory — into his tray, and ran,
Entering the waves of the stadium like a drowning man.
Poor Billy Rose. God, he could fight
Before my three sharp coins knocked out his sight.

Space Miner

for Robert Morgan

His face was a map of traces where veins
Had exploded bleeding in atmospheres too
Frail to hold that life, and scar tissue
Hung soft as pads where his cheekbones shone
Under the skin when he was young.
He had worked deep seams where encrusted ore,
Too tight for his diamond drill, had ripped
Strips from his flesh. Dust from a thousand metals
Silted his lungs and softened the strength
Of his muscles. He had worked the treasuries
Of many near stars, but now he stood on the moving
Pavement reserved for cripples who had served well.
The joints of his hands were dry and useless
Under the cold gloves issued by the government.

Before they brought his sleep in a little capsule
He would look through the hospital window
At the ships of young men bursting into space.
For this to happen he had worked till his body broke.
Now they flew to the farthest worlds in the universe:
Mars, Eldorado, Mercury, Earth, Saturn.

Gardening Gloves

Mild, knob-jointed, old,
They lie on the garage floor.
Scarred by the turn of a spade
In hard, agricultural wear
And soiled by seasonal mould
They *look* like animal skins —
Or imagine a gargoyle's hands.

But not my hands I'd swear,
Being large, rough and uncouth;
Yet the moment I pick them up
They assume an absurd truth,
They assert I have given them shape,
Making my hands the mirror
For their comfortable horror.

And I know if I put them on
I gain a deliberate skill,
An old, slow satisfaction
That is not mine at all
But sent down from other men.
Yes, dead men live again
In my reluctant skin.

I remember my father's hands,
How they moved as mine do now
While he took his jokes from the air
Like precise, comical birds.
These gloves are my proper wear.
We all preserve such lives.
I'm not sorry to have these gloves.

Barn Owl

Ernie Morgan found him, a small
Fur mitten inexplicably upright,
And hissing like a treble kettle
Beneath the tree he'd fallen from.
His bright eye frightened Ernie,
Who popped a rusty bucket over him
And ran for us. We kept him
In a backyard shed, perched
On the rung of a broken deck-chair,
Its canvas faded to his down's biscuit.
Men from the pits, their own childhood
Spent waste in the crippling earth,
Held him gently, brought him mice
From the wealth of our riddled tenements,
Saw that we understood his tenderness,
His tiny body under its puffed quilt,
Then left us alone. We called him Snowy.

He was never clumsy. He flew
From the first like a skilled moth,
Sifting the air with feathers,
Floating it softly to the place he wanted.
At dusk he'd stir, preen, stand
At the window-ledge, fly. It was
A catching of the heart to see him go.
Six months we kept him, saw him
Grow beautiful in a way each thought
His own knowledge. One afternoon, home
With pretended illness, I watched him
Leave. It was daylight. He lifted slowly
Over the Hughes's roof, his cream face calm,
And never came back. I saw this;
And tell it for the first time,
Having wanted to keep his mystery.

And would not say it now, but that
This morning, walking in Slindon woods
Before the sun, I found a barn owl
Dead in the rusty bracken.
He was not clumsy in his death,
His wings folded decently to him,
His plumes, unruffled orange,
Bore flawlessly their delicate patterning.
With a stick I turned him, not
Wishing to touch his feathery stiffness.
There was neither blood nor wound on him,
But for the savaged foot a scavenger
Had ripped. I saw the sinews.
I could have skewered them out
Like a common fowl's. Moving away
I was oppressed by him, thinking
Confusedly that down the generations
Of air this death was Snowy's
Emblematic messenger, that I should know
The meaning of it, the dead barn owl.

Burning the Bracken

When summer stopped, and the last
Lit cloud blazed tawny cumulus
Above the hills, it was the bracken

Answered; its still crests
Contained an autumn's burning.
Then, on an afternoon of promised

Cold, true flames ripped
The ferns. Hurrying fire, low
And pale in the sun, ran

Glittering through them. As
Night fell, the brindle
Flambeaux, full of chattering

We were too far to hear, leapt
To the children's singing.
'Fire on the mountain,' we

Chanted, who went to bed warmed
By joy. But I would know that fires
Die, that the cold sky holds

Uneasily the fronds and floating
Twigs of broken soot, letting
Them fall, fall now, soft

As darkness on this white page.

Elegy for David Beynon

David, we must have looked comic, sitting
there at next desks; your legs stretched
half-way down the classroom, while
my feet hung a free inch above

the floor. I remember, too, down
at The Gwynne's Field, at the side
of the little Taff, dancing with
laughing fury as you caught

effortlessly at the line-out, sliding
the ball over my head direct to
the outside-half. That was Cyril
Theophilus, who died in his quiet

so long ago that only I, perhaps,
remember he'd hold the ball one-handed
on his thin stomach as he turned
to run. Even there you were careful

to miss us with your scattering
knees as you bumped through
for yet another try. Buffeted
we were, but cheered too by our

unhurt presumption in believing
we could ever have pulled you down.
I think those children, those who died
under your arms in the crushed school,

would understand that I make this
your elegy. I know the face you had,
have walked with you enough mornings
under the fallen leaves. Theirs is

the great anonymous tragedy one word
will summarise. Aberfan, I write it
for them here, knowing we've paid to it
our shabby pence, and now it can be stored

with whatever names there are where
children end their briefest pilgrimage.
I cannot find the words for you, David. These
are too long, too many; and not enough.

Christmas Day

Winter drought, and a parched wind
Roughens the mud. Wrapped in a parka,
Leaning leaky into the slack
The blast misses as it screams over

The blackthorn, I'm tramping a
Chalk ditch from the downs. Leaves
Dry as cornflakes crack under
My gumboots, the hedge is against

My shoulder. Sand of their flying
Dusts hunt the spent fields, ice
Grains stick at my eyes. Caught
On the thorns, a rip of newsprint

Shivers its yellow edges, grows
Long, then rises easily, a narrow
Heron, out of shadow. It rises,
Trailing its thin legs, into cold

Sun flat as the land. Upright,
Broad wings spread, neck curved
And head and great blade turned
Down on the lit breast, it hangs

Against barbs, against winter
Darkness, before its slow vanes
Beat once over the elms, a
Christ crucified, a flying Christ.

John Ormond

John Ormond was born in 1923 in Dunvant, Swansea. After an early career as a journalist he then went on to spend some years as a documentary film maker for the BBC where his subjects included Dylan Thomas, Alun Lewis, Vernon Watkins and R.S. Thomas. He died in 1990. Seren published his *Selected Poems* in 1987.

My Grandfather and his Apple Tree

Life sometimes held such sweetness for him
As to engender guilt. From the night vein he'd come,
From working in water wrestling the coal,
Up the pit slant. Every morning hit him
Like a journey of trams between the eyes;
A wild and drinking farmboy sobered by love
Of a miller's daughter and a whitewashed cottage
Suddenly to pay rent for. So he'd left the farm
For dark under the fields six days a week
With mandrel and shovel and different stalls.
All light was beckoning. Soon his hands
Untangled a brown garden into neat greens.

There was an apple tree he limed, made sturdy;
The fruit was sweet and crisp upon the tongue
Until it budded temptation in his mouth.
Now he had given up whistling on Sundays,
Attended prayer-meetings, added a concordance
To his wedding Bible and ten children
To the village population. He nudged the line,

Clean-pinafored and collared, glazed with soap,
Every seventh day of rest in Ebenezer;
Shaved on a Saturday night to escape the devil.

The sweetness of the apples worried him.
He took a branch of cooker from a neighbour
When he became deacon, wanting
The best of both his worlds. Clay from the colliery
He thumbed about the bole one afternoon
Grafting the sour to sweetness, bound up
The bleeding white of junction with broad strips
Of working flannel-shirt and belly-bands
To join the two in union. For a time
After the wound healed the sweetness held,
The balance tilted towards an old delight.

But in the time that I remember him
(His wife had long since died, I never saw her)
The sour half took over. Every single apple
Grew — across twenty Augusts — bitter as wormwood.
He'd sit under the box tree, his pink gums
(Between the white moustache and goatee beard)
Grinding thin slices that his jack-knife cut,
Sucking for sweetness vainly. It had gone,
Gone. I heard him mutter
Quiet Welsh oaths as he spat the gall-juice
Into the seeding onion-bed, watched him toss
The big core into the spreading nettles.

Froga

Two yew trees sentried his black garden gate
And every summer Sunday night
He stood between them, a general
Of misery, inspecting them and
The bad joke of the world,

His uniform a black suit, mildew green;
His black velour hat verdigrised round the band
From his sweat at life's jaundice.
His eyebrows were black moustaches,
His moustache the prototype
Of all those worn by practitioners
In the old ambulance books
Where the patient's beyond repair,
But his eyes not evil, rather
The eyes of a dying seal in a bankrupt circus.

Only once did I hear him speak, to scare
Off a blackbird that sang in his yew-tree.
Behind his back we called him Froga,
Half frog, half ogre.

I heard say that they buried him in his suit;
They didn't think it would burn:
And that in his coffin, because they'd taken out
His teeth, he lay there smiling.

Design for a Quilt

First let there be a tree, roots taking ground
In bleached and soft blue fabric.
Into the well-aired sky branches extend
Only to bend away from the turned-back
Edge of linen where day's horizons end;

Branches symmetrical, not over-flaunting
Their leaves (let ordinary swansdown
Be their lining), which in the summertime
Will lie lightly upon her, the girl
This quilt's for, this object of designing;

But such too, when deep frosts veneer
Or winds prise at the slates above her,
Or snows lie in the yard in a black sulk,

That the embroidered cover, couched
And applied with pennants of green silk,

Will still be warm enough that should she stir
To draw a further foliage about her
The encouraged shoots will quicken
And, at her breathing, midnight's spring
Can know new season as they thicken.

Feather-stitch on every bough
A bird, one neat French-knot its eye,
To sing a silent night-long lullaby
And not disturb her or disbud her.
See that the entwining motives run

In and about themselves to bring
To bed the sheens and mossy lawns of Eden;
For air would have a perfect thing
To echo if not equal Paradise
As garden for her true temptation:

So that in future times, recalling
The pleasures of past falling, she'll bequeath it
To one or other of the line,
Bearing her name or mine,
With luck I'll help her make beneath it.

Cathedral Builders

They climbed on sketchy ladders towards God,
With winch and pulley hoisted hewn rock into heaven,
Inhabited sky with hammers, defied gravity,
Deified stone, took up God's house to meet Him,

And came down to their suppers and small beer;
Every night slept, lay with their smelly wives,
Quarrelled and cuffed the children, lied,
Spat, sang, were happy or unhappy,

And every day took to the ladders again;
Impeded the rights of way of another summer's
Swallows, grew greyer, shakier, became less inclined
To fix a neighbour's roof of a fine evening,

Saw naves sprout arches, clerestories soar,
Cursed the loud fancy glaziers for their luck,
Somehow escaped the plague, got rheumatism,
Decided it was time to give it up,

To leave the spire to others; stood in the crowd
Well back from the vestments at the consecration,
Envied the fat bishop his warm boots,
Cocked up a squint eye and said, 'I bloody did that'.

Lament for a Leg

Near the yew tree under which the body of Dafydd ap Gwilym is buried in Strata Florida, Cardiganshire, there stands a stone with the following inscription: 'The left leg and part of the thigh of Henry Hughes, Cooper, was cut off and interr'd here, June 18, 1756'. Later the rest of Henry Hughes set off across the Atlantic in search of better fortune.

A short service, to be sure,
With scarcely half a hymn they held,
over my lost limb, suitable curtailment.
Out-of-tune notes a crow cawed
By the yew tree, and me,
My stump still tourniquéd,
Awkward on my new crutch,
Being snatched towards the snack
Of a funeral feast they made.
With seldom a dry eye, for laughter,
They jostled me over the ale
I'd cut the casks for, and the mead.
'Catch me falling under a coach,'
Every voice jested, save mine,
Henry Hughes, cooper. A tasteless caper!
Soon with my only, my best, foot forward
I fled, quiet, to far America:

Where, with my two tried hands, I plied
My trade and true, in time made good
Though grieving for Pontrhydfendigaid.
Sometimes, all at once, in my tall cups,
I'd cry in *hiraeth* for my remembered thigh
Left by the grand yew in Ystrad Fflur's
Bare ground, near the good bard.
Strangers, astonished at my high
Beer-flush, would stare, not guessing,
Above the bar-board, that I, of the starry eye,
Had one foot in the grave; thinking me
No doubt, a drunken dolt in whom a whim
Warmed to madness, not knowing a tease
Of a Welsh worm was tickling my distant toes.

'So I bequeath my leg,' I'd say and sigh,
Baffling them, 'my unexiled part, to Dafydd
The pure poet who, whole, lies near and far
From me, still pining for Morfudd's heart,'
Giving him, generous to a fault
With what was no more mine to give,
Out of that curt plot, my quarter grave,
Good help, I hope. What will the great God say
At Dafydd's wild-kicking-climbing extra leg,
Jammed hard in heaven's white doorway
(I'll limp unnimble round the narrow back)
Come the quick trumpet of the Judgement Day?

Landscape in Dyfed
for Graham Sutherland

Because the sea grasped cleanly here, and there
Coaxed too unsurely until clenched strata
Resisted, an indecision of lanes resolves
This land into gestures of beckoning
Towards what is here and beyond, and both at hand.

Walk where you will, below is an estuary.
In advance to a fleeting brightness you traverse
So many shoals of the dead who have drowned
In stone, so many hibernations
Of souls, you could be in phantom country.

But the tapers of gorse burn slowly, otherwise.
And here are rock cathedrals which can be
As small as your span. And, at the water's edge,
A struck havoc of trees clutches the interim season,
The given roots bare, seeming to feed on the wind;

And in their limbs what compass of sun
Is contained, what sealed apparitions of summer,
What transfixed ambulations. If you could cut
Right to the heart and uncouple the innermost rings
Beyond those nerves you would see the structure of air.

The Birth of Venus at Aberystwyth

Beyond the pier varicose waves crocheted
A complex permanent nothing on the stones.
The Corporation deck-chairs flapped
Haphazard unison. Most sea-front windows

Confessed to Vacancies; and on the promenade
A violinist in Scotch-plaid dinner-jacket
Contributed little to the Welsh way of life
As he played 'Thanks for the Memory'

To two small children and a dog. Without
Any expectation at all, the sea brandished
Its vanity. The one-eyed coastguard was dozing.
Nothing in the sky sought a response.

The occasional pebble moved, gave itself back
To the perpetual, casual disorder

Of all perfectly-shaped, meaningless forms,
Like pebbles. There was one beachcomber,

From Basingstoke, but he noticed nothing
Unusual either when far out, beyond
The beginning of the ninth (one could even
Go as far as to say the ninetieth) wave,

Dolphins who hadn't spoken to each other
For years formed squadrons for her.
Trenches of water broke open, deep
Where she was, coming up. Weeds fandangoed,

Currents changed their course. Inside
An instant's calm her hair began to float,
Marbling the hollows like old ledgers.
The sea still tells the story in its own

Proud language, but few understand it;
And, as you may imagine, the beauty of it is lost
In the best translations available....
Her different world was added to the world

As, nearing shore, sensing something dubious,
Something fishy in the offing, the dolphin-fleet
Turned back. The lady nearly drowned,
But hobbled in, grazing her great toe.

Do not ask questions about where she came from
Or what she was, or what colour was her hair;
Though there are reasons for supposing
That, when it dried, its light took over

Where the summer left off. The following Sunday
She wore a safe beige hat for morning service
At the Baptist Church. Even so, the minister
Ignored her as she left, and she didn't go again.

Gwyn Parry

Gwyn Parry was born in 1961 in Bangor and raised in Anglesey. His recent Seren collection, *Mynydd Parys*, is based on an old copper mine situated near Amlwch on the north coast of Anglesey and is accompanied by Steve Makin's photographs. Gwyn now lives and works in Dublin.

His Graveyard

I watched him tonight
Waltzing with his sharp partner,
Relentlessly swaying and
Slaying tall seed grass.
His eye full of sunlight
And the sound of the *wialen ogi*.

He is a snake
With a scythe tongue
Moving between his friends' graves.
The scythe swings
In the arc of his world;
Exposing slow-worms and toads
To a setting summer night.

He sits for a smoke
On a headstone.
Moths lands on his shirt.
Horseflies suck his blood.

Mynydd Parys

On yellow bone rock
I establish my foothold.

I throw stones
into the fish-mouth hole,
no closer I will fall

I draw my finger
through the softness
of sulphur.

I handle rocks,
splendid in their colours
like tropical fish.

I know a way inside,
a shoulder-width hole,
I avoid its socket of black.

I climb to the glitter
of iron and zinc,
sit on a zebra-striped rock.

I watch the sun anoint
the tallest spoil-heap

watch it roll down the light
of the afternoon.

Miner's Candle

I have a candle
that has not been lit
for a hundred years.

I found it under the sun,
lodged in a stone.

I put my hand on it
like it was meant.

I found it near a shaft
forty-five feet in diameter,
re-opened
like a black purse.

June

River cuts the estuary
like a cool knife,

crows scatter circles
burnt bonfire papers

they rise
on the wind's warm finger.

Red Kite
on his scavenge

folding a central hinge
wings lapping his side.

Silence
lives in this place

an eyeless farm
in a tin sky.

Out at sea
God thunders his hot drum.

Richard Poole

Richard Poole was born in Bradford on New Year's Day, 1945. He has two degrees from UCNW Bangor and has been a tutor in English for some years at Coleg Harlech. He is author of *Richard Hughes: Novelist* and four collections of poetry. He was editor of *Poetry Wales* magazine from 1992-96.

Words before Midnight

Our son lies drowned in deep seas of sleep.
It is impossible to tell what dream-things
inhabit him. His breathing is so light
I cannot think it inconvenient
to the evanescent business of the air.

He would be thus in death — but with the absence
of this faint rose-bloom from his cheeks.
That is what most of all I could not bear.
Even to imagine it quickens a sour
shudder along my heart. But what put death there?

Love, let's go to bed. At a time such as this
the desire I feel for you cannot be told
from my need. But I need not importune
what you will grant without giving me,
that which I shall seize surrendering.

And now, desiring spent, we lie back
in not unamicable darkness,
mimics of the makers of the child
in the next room, to whom, indiscriminate,
we gave uncertain life, certain death.

These Bracken-roots

inhabit a packed, granular, sleeving sea —
a soil half sand with drowned knurrs of stone.

Nothing else that lives can live with them:
other radices cramp in the loam-shallows.

In spring the fern-roots thrust up to the sun,
each blunt, relentless tip the palest green.

Sap-veins in a planet-skin, the dun roots
consolidate their network imperceptibly —

till spade and fork contest supremacy,
disbranch and bruise that multiple singleness.

Ripped from their element, stranded above ground
the roots desiccate. The air dyes them black.

Back

        The clock ticks on — swift
imperturbable time recording itself.
Returning from elsewhere
to selves which recognize these things
we come back, back gradually,
drawn again to the process by the mind's
tyrannical will to know itself.

Now, in this lucid aftermath,
the realm of sense we visited seems already
a marvellous island obscured by a soft haze.
So love, remember this: flesh contains
its own transcendent, and time — which stops
all love and murders every lover —
        is only stopped by love.

Sheenagh Pugh

Sheenagh Pugh was born in Birmingham in 1950. A graduate of the University of Bristol in Russian and German, she is the author of seven collections of poetry including 1990's well-received *Selected Poems*. She currently lives in Cardiff and lectures at the University of Glamorgan. Her last book was *Sing for the Taxman*. Her next volume, *ID'S HOSPIT*, will appear in 1997.

Intercity Lullaby

They're both what, nineteen? Their dark hair
flops: they've had a long day on the beer,
or the travel, sitting slumped in sleep,
each with his feet cradled in the other's lap.

Balulalow, beautiful tired boys,
and if I could, I would give you the choice
of where to spend your lives, and what to do:
you should not so be shuttled to and fro.

Newcastle United black and white
on their bags: they'll be in London tonight,
looking to find the streets paved with brass;
fairy tales are practical, nowadays.

Balow marras, balow canny lads,
and if I could, I would rebuild your trades
and let you play at home all seasons long
at doing what you liked, and being young.

Two stations back, they were talking about
the fair at Whitley Bay, while they ate
the food their mothers packed, just before
waving them off to look for their adventure.

Lullay innocents: lully, lully, lullay,
and if I could, I would make away
the witch: break spells, change the frog-prince's shape,
shut down the engine's noise to guard your sleep.

The Black Beach
Skogarstrand, South Iceland

Nobody told us it was going to be black.
Day at the beach, see the puffins, fine,
and there it was,
                    black.
                         Not streaked with coal,
nor shaly, nor polluted; just pure ash

as fine as sand, running through our hands
and leaving no mark where we looked to see
a sooty smudge; uncanny, like a man
without footprints. The sea creamed in,

bone-white, startling; edging with lace
the black velvet. You could have sat down,
but no one did; no-one picnicked or made
sand-pies of the stuff. It was beautiful,

really beautiful, that stretch of darkness,
but people trod on it as if they were walking
over their graves. A seal's shining head
surfaced close; seemed to look; then sheered off.

Exhibition

He's playing trick shots to entertain
the crowd, because the match finished early.
And why was that? He was comprehensively
hammered, that's why; he didn't win

a frame. Now it's all going well:
now it doesn't matter, he can knock
them in from anywhere. There's a wisecrack
from the audience; he looks a bit pale,

small wonder, but he's right in there
fighting back, turning the laugh, as if
no-one just hurt most of the life
out of him for some hours. He's a master

now, showing them how to do it,
the skills of which most of us just dream,
courage, class, humour. That's the game
in the end, and he's a player all right.

Spring '72

Now open flowers on the shirts of boys;
now mica glistens, asphalt's morning dew,
from pavements up. Now all the girls look pregnant,
and small red sports cars blossom on the streets.

Now all birds are not sparrows; now all women
unwrap their shapes from winter. Now the man
who thought it might be fun to walk to work
finds all sight aches, all touch troubles his blood.

Now all the state of opening, upspring, bud's
soft burst, a green grenade, scrapes at his grief;
now all the many dead dress him in black
for what they had and what he cannot keep.

from *Earth Studies*
'Do you think we'll ever get to see earth, sir?'

I hear they're hoping to run trips
one day, for the young and fit, of course.
I don't see much use in it myself;
there'll be any number of places
you can't land, because they're still toxic,
and even in the relatively safe bits
you won't see what it was; what it could be.
I can't fancy a tour through the ruins
of my home with a party of twenty-five
and a guide to tell me what to see.
But if you should see some beautiful thing,
some leaf, say, damascened with frost,
some iridescence on a pigeon's neck,
some stone, some curve, some clear water;
look at it as if you were made of eyes,
as if you were nothing but an eye, lidless
and tender, to be probed and scorched
by extreme light. Look at it with your skin,
with the small hairs on the back of your neck.
If it is well-shaped, look at it with your hands;
if it has fragrance, breathe it into yourself;
if it tastes sweet, put your tongue to it.
Look at it as a happening, a moment;
let nothing of it go unrecorded,
map it as if it were already passing.
Look at it with the inside of your head,
look at it for later, look at it for ever,
and look at it once for me.

She was nineteen, and she was bored

She was nineteen, and she was bored
with being a kitchenmaid, cleaning a house,
being nobody. She joined the murderous crew
of mediocrities out on the loose

246

after revenge. They gave her a uniform
and high black riding-boots; no housemaid's gear,
and a whip, and enough authority
to look in most faces and see fear.

She was head wardress; she had the word,
people lived or died at her option,
and mostly died, because, given power,
she overdosed on the exhilaration

of misusing it, of seeing her betters
at her boots: where's your brains now, eh,
your education, your class, your fancy job,
your money? She spent five years on a high.

She could have followed other roads to fame:
she might have been a heroine, a Joan,
she might have been noted for character
or wit, or courage, or compassion,

if she'd been intelligent, large-minded,
but she was neither; she was a failure
born and bred; an ignorant slut, which didn't stop her
being dissatisfied, taking what adventure

she saw. She was hanged young, as she deserved,
it's no excuse that she did what we might.
Those who made her world are still in business:
the likes of her are no nearer the light.

Remember, Remember

This slumped bag of rags in the barrow
isn't him: this sad clown's turniphead
not my tall soldier, my November hero,
my ruined sunlight. He has been dead

so long now: young, he fills my eyes,
but the children make him an old man
in their play; drag him begging for pennies
till fire twists his face, and he dies again.

I saw his face when he died the first time,
the thin paper with the bones' motif
traced through it. There was nothing of him:
he swayed on the scaffold like a leaf

in autumn. Now the day of thanksgiving
for his death blows the boys out of school,
scatters their laughter. And the birds are leaving;
the wind tosses them in a white handful

at the heavy sky. Trees against the dark
burn: there's a young beech, leaves just kindled
gold at the edges, but the big oak
blazes yellow, and the rowan's red

crackles and glows. The old man who stands
in the wind's stream, letting the shreds of light
fly around him, might be warming his hands
at the fire, before the year goes out.

But the boys stacking their wood so high
don't guess that death will have to do with them.
When they start the blaze, it will go quickly:
a few hours to feast their eyes on flame,

before the white ash settles, and the man
of rags, the sacrifice, topples and dies.
My soldier once told me the world would burn
before we parted, but it was otherwise:

it burns each year, and never licks the fringe
of the dark in me, growing like the fir
that is always black out; that does not change
for autumn's light, nor the white sky of winter.

Sometimes

Sometimes things don't go, after all,
from bad to worse. Some years, muscadel
faces down frost; green thrives; the crops don't fail,
sometimes a man aims high, and all goes well.

A people sometimes will step back from war;
elect an honest man; decide they care
enough, that they can't leave some stranger poor.
Some men become what they were born for.

Sometimes our best efforts do not go
amiss, sometimes we do as we meant to.
The sun will sometimes melt a field of sorrow
that seemed hard frozen: may it happen for you.

The Embarkation of the Pigs

*on hearing that british publishers no longer
welcome pig characters in children's books*

Piglet can take a hint. He walks off
page four, leaving a small white space
among the swirling snowflakes. Pooh wanders on,
his paw grasping at air, toward the place

where the Hundred Acre merges into Nutwood,
and Rupert stares at a Podgy-shaped gap.
Meanwhile, houses of brick, sticks and straw
open their doors, and out the Three step,

in their trotters. At every turn,
some other joins the band: on some page
a word fades. They follow Pigling Bland
down to the pea-green boat at the tide's edge,

that will take them to the eternal wood
where the Piggywig stands; where the round moon
will countenance their portly, tolerant curves.
This is where outlaws dance. Shine on; shine on.

Deryn Rees-Jones

Deryn Rees-Jones was born in Liverpool in 1968 and has lived in Bangor and London. She is currently completing a book on post-war women's poetry, *Consorting with Angels*, for Bloodaxe and reviews regularly for *London Magazine*. Her debut Seren collection, *The Memory Tray*, was shortlisted for a Forward Prize.

Lovesong to Captain James T. Kirk

Captain. I never thought we'd come to this,
but things being what they are, being adults,
stardate '94 it's best to make the best of it
and laugh. What's done is done. Perhaps
I'll start to call you Jim or Jamie, James....

No one was more shocked than me when I arrived
(the lady doth protest) to find
my bruised and rainy planet disappeared
and me, materialised and reconstructed
on board the Starship Enterprise, all 60s
with my lacquered bee-hive and my thigh-high
skirt in blue, my Doctor Marten's and my jeans
replaced by skin-tight boots
and scratchy blue-black nylons rippling-
up my less-than-perfect calves. Sulu
looked worried. Spock cocked up one eyebrow
enigmatically, branding my existence
'perfectly illogical'. How nice, I thought. His ears.
Uhura smiled of course, and fiddled

with her hair. O James. Truth is
I loved you even as a child...

O slick-black-panted wanderer holding
your belly in, your phaser gun
on stun, and eyes like Conference pears! You're not my type
but I undress you, and we fuck
and I forgive your pancake make-up and mascara,
the darker shadows painted round your eyes.
The lava-lamp goes up and down. We're
a strange unison. Politically
Mismatched. Our mutual friend
The Doc takes notes. 'Go easy Bones!'
Scotty is beaming and shouts 'Energise',
and all of a sudden you remind me
Of my dad, my brother and my mum,
my body rising like a shadow from the past
on top of you. As I press your arms behind your head
I drape my breasts so that you
brush my nipples gently with your lips almost
involuntarily as we boldly go. Come slowly, Captain,
and we do, with both our pairs of eyes tight closed.

Grandma in the Garden

Fence — a thousand little crucifixions,
Stays to the garden:
It's holding its breath

As weeds, the arrogant subversives, contemplate
Their birth. The grass

Is slightly anxious, its green
Unshaven head tremulous

With indecision, beckoning the poplars
To formal disarray, but

They won't come any closer, of that
We can be sure.

The pond smiles, a green ironic
Smear — gruesome as

Overcooked vegetables, pushed
To the side: ridiculous.

O fishes fishes fishes?
They have not swum for twenty years

And their corpses are not welcome here.
We must avert our eyes

To the wild dwarf roses in the rockery
Which sit, autistic, unafraid.

Draped elegantly in fuchsia and in black
Here Grandma watches from a chair,

One wild Modigliani eye hooking
The clouds, and lost

In the terrible gap between grass
And sky that the children know,
That they put in their pictures.

Metamorphoses

In examining the earliest mental shapes assumed by the sexual life of children we have been in the habit of taking as the subject of investigations the male child, the little boy. With little girls, so we have supposed, things must be similar, though in some way or other they must nevertheless be different. Freud - *Some Psychical Consequences of the Anatomical Differences Between the Sexes*

No one believes I'm Marilyn Monroe, 36-28-36. At fifty,
5'10, a beard and thirteen stone, not even me. But you have to dream.

A Girl Can't Help It. I think of her like nothing else:
Her breasts. A strip of thigh. The way a body moves. *Love Goddess.*
Her teeth like buttons on an open shirt. Her prawn-pink lips.
That mole. And her face like a white flower, blossoming, blossoming.
Her heels tap out my destiny. A sexy, breathy tune. I want
To step out from this body like a snake would lose its skin.

My shrink wears wigs and slacks. I wear a yellow dress, have polish
On my fingernails. She speaks in baritone, Butch to my *Femme.* My legs
Cross at the ankle, hers the knee. More of a man than me.
I wanted a couch I could lie right back on. A vase of lilies,
Or Egyptian artefacts. A way I could explain myself.
My self. My. Self. Instead an upright chair. A large-spooled
                                        tape-machine.
The window ladling the sunlight like syrup from a tin. My eyes
A glass of water, shrinking on the window sill...

She made me watch The Op. on video, the curtains drawn. Where
Parts of Me would go. Adjustments. Hormones. Sutures. Scars. It
                                        changes
Nips and Tucks alright. The canopies of flesh. No going back. Making me
Question everything. I cried. Considering myself in terms of pain.
                                        Just like
Bereavement. Moving house. Divorce. Or finding a new name. The
                                        endless re-
Arrangements. Three years later and I find (excuse the cliché, please)
                                        I'm
Falling in love again. The woman I once married. Her tears
As sticky-sweet as candyfloss. Her ordinary beauty makes me pale.

She says she loves me and she likes it. Hot. The little places
Where I've learned to push my tongue. Her two hands brush my breasts
Like angel wings. Like tiny falling stars. Her mouth. The way I feel it

Here. The space between us changes shape each night,
Opens and closes — kaleidoscopic loops and whirls. Sometimes
Diamonds Are a Girl's Best Friend. You know? *Boop-Boop-Be-Doop.*
Our joke. And *Happy Birthday.* Marilyn. Last night, as perfect
Yet more perfect than a wedding ring — our bodies rising,
Falling. There, growing between us, an exquisitely shaped O.

Don Rodgers

Don Rodgers was born in London in 1957 and educated at Oxford. His prizewinning poetry has been published in a number of magazines and anthologies. Author of published short stories as well as plays, he lives and works in Swansea. His debut Seren collection is *Moontan*.

Keys

Nothing cuts like the teeth of keys.
They lobotomize brick;
break and enter cloisters;
tinker with tabernacles, hearts, minds;
saw through shadows;
chew through the safest sex;
screw you out of doors, into corridors;
corrugate the smoothest, silkiest skin.

Keys poke their thin noses into everything,
insatiably: pry, prise, surprise;
they keep on digging deeper, egging themselves in;
like spies, they're always first behind the enemy lines.

And when they get together, like old boys,
how they bore the pants off you,
with their jaw-jaw, and their haw-haw,
their jingoistic jangling;
while they uglily bulge in all the wrong places;
or flaunt their plastic tags like old Etonian ties.

Hung up they're no better.
One's a weapon.
Two's mechanical sin.
Three's an inscrutable syllogism of bones.
More's a bunch: of iron, embittered laughs.

God, how I hate keys; though I love locks.
Keys cut me up.

Ferns in a Welsh Valley

This valley is full of relics.
Atop the steep slopes, the castle
has been ruined by time, its keep unkept,
its large square stones heavily overgrown.

Out of this castle, one fine day,
came lords and ladies, knights and squires,
descending into the wooded valley.

You can still see them here in the ferns,
ranked luxuriantly one above the other,
their soft shields, broad bucklers, and rusty backs
swayed over by the tasselled heads of kings.

See how the ladies link their fingers with the fronds of males,
their maiden hair in decorous disarray on the damp rocks,
while the tongues of faithful harts lap at their feet.

Sometimes, when a small wind stirs,
you can hear them murmur of their conquests and misdeeds,
sighing, as more and more of their tight fists
uncurl, and the soft green chains of their bodies open.

Now they are breathing out in long, synchronous waves,
scattering the gold dust of their histories
into a future they feel for, but cannot see.

Château Lamouche

A fly is a hairy-fairy, incongruous creature
of alien appearance and habits.
It walks upside down on the ceiling
with black looks like a spider.

It has too many legs to be friendly, sees four dimensions;
like a grand master, is at least one step ahead:
however much you practise that deadpan face
it will always beat you to the draw.

A fly can see the whites of your eyes a mile off;
it smells decay, homing in on you, like a pallid stinkhorn —
you flinch, brush it away, quickly, or it might bite,
syringe you full of some dreadful disease like sleeping
                                                    sickness.

Wailing gleefully, flies congregate greedily on death;
for them, the most impregnable integument's a thin skin;
a dead dog or Welshman's a home of breeding, a castle,
                                    barraqué,
coulant, with an elegantly overblown bouquet:
                                    Château Lamouche.

A fly's a pig: it spits on its food, and walks on goo,
but is impossible to give a name to, or domesticate.
It lays inedible eggs, like the white heads of pustules;
it isn't squeamish in the least, making maggots by the million.

Sometimes you catch it thinking it's quite cute, cleaning dainty
deltawings, and flashing its blue arse at you in the sun.
Happy with life, it hums when you're half asleep, or
shakes itself, like a miniature maraca, against the window-pane.

Flies sing when they die, all on one note, uncomprehendingly;
their private parts are unimaginable, their sex indeterminable.
Above all, they fly: they've taken over their names; while we
manage it only in dreams, kicking against the pricks, like the
                                    hanged.

256

When killing flies,
you should do it quickly, blindly, like a suicide,
before you can say 'Gloucester', or *'Calliphora vomitoria'*,
or read what they've inked, in black and blue, on your soft
white walls.

A fly's a small siren; it's unsafe for your peace of mind
to look one in the face; if you do,
you'll see yourself reticulate, chromatically decompose
to facets of two huge, entrancing eyes.

Pearl Everlasting

This plant is called the Pearl Everlasting.
Its buds are papery pearls, clasping
stiff gold flowers.

Drops of water are balanced beautifully
on the long silvered leaves
like diamonds on knives.

Such plants are precious in the Rhondda.
You don't have to sift for these pearls:
the sky, the hacked hillsides, are their open oyster.

Today, grey clouds have come and gone, like
officials on a conducted tour: waves
of ferns are bowing and scraping in their wake.

Now evening bruises the valley a soft blue.
While the Pearl Everlasting flowers
on regardless amongst the plane rock splinters.

Above it, on a sheer cliff face,
someone's daubed in fresh white paint:
REMEMBER THE LORD THY GOD ALL THY DAYS.

Frances Sackett

Frances Sackett was born in Chirk in 1948 and lived in Wales throughout her childhood. She recently completed a postgraduate degree in literature at the University of Manchester and now lives near Manchester with her family where she works in a bookshop. Her new debut Seren collection is *The Hand Glass*.

Vanity

After a painting by F.C. Cowper 1877-1958

The painter wanted embellishments,
What else could I do but dream and admire?
The props had never been so interesting,
Turning my cheeks to fire, filling the hand-glass
With a multitude of flashes, that flew like
Jolted planets, across the scanty sky of cloth
Set up behind.

        Such a change from angel-white —
The sultry taffeta, brocade in chains
Like gilded snakes that swarmed my arms,
My hands so formally arranged
To show the rings and touch the pearls
That wound their way around my neck,
Then trailed and looped against
The silken chair.

        And so he calls me 'Vanity'
And makes me feel the guilt of all
His observation. I only bared my shoulders

Once before, and that was when
A boy I loved said beauty lay
In what was unadorned.

Change of Weather at Conwy

Chimney-smoke curling from slate roofs
Then blowing out seaward like a squall.
Sky lightening momentarily — magnolia-petalled,
Shifting a sifting of cloud against castle parapets
(A feather-light caress as flesh warms on flesh)
And pouring a prism of yellow
Laser-angled at Deganwy.
(Caught in the glow and melting within sunlit rooms.)

Gulls standing sentinel, spanning
Turret, quay and quiff of a wave,
(From stronghold to height in rhythm with the sea)
Their cries echoing history through dank castle walls
Of battles fought in fervour — now extinguished.
(Enmeshed, entangled, abandoned in sheer exhaustion
Like nets along the quay.)

The Walled Orchard

The walled orchard tingles
With the remnants of rain
Wind-rushed in the treetops.
Tiny carmine apples dangle
Beads of rain like teats.
Carnations circle a stone
Like an exposed eye ball—
A pool of water in its cave-hole
Muddy and mossed,
Deep as an iris.
One tree with a flick of blossom —
A tiny pink bud with wings.

259

Snap-dragons rooted through mortar
Like foot-holds,
Stencilling the old, pink brick.
Now the rank stink of vegetation
Pours from the earth,
Fuchsias drip red-painted fingernails
Over the bench,
Rain begins again
Swarming in the treetops.

A Way of Looking

Once I'd seen them that way
It was hard to imagine ordinary lives
In overcrowded tenements.
Precarious pillars of light —
Ephemeral in the haze across the bay.
We had to wait for evening to see them best;
They emerged from the rosy sky like
Athenian columns, decadent, not of this world.

But when we went up close
And saw the washing flap
From every flaking balcony
And not a Grecian god in sight
I wanted motes to cloud my eyes.

I'll always see them both ways
But know the frail ephemeral image
Is like imagination in the distance
That sometimes seems remote
And out of grasp.
But only waits for light to change
And then emerges slowly into focus,
Or in a flash is sudden and serene.

Graham Thomas

Born in 1944 in Abertillery and educated at UCW Aberystwyth, Graham Thomas returned to teach in Gwent where for some years he was Head of Science at Abertillery School. He has now retired. His Seren volume is *The One Place*.

A Frog

Came into the school one day
Out of the long grass at the back,
Another on the trail that brought us
Sheep and ponies from the hill,
Mice from the hayfield, rabbits, cats,
And a long line of dogs from the houses above
Restless and shivering in the wind
Till end-of-lesson bells. This one
I wouldn't have known was there, except
For all the noise outside my room —
Choruses of shrieks and catcalls,
Sounds fierce enough to hurt, to kill,
Then only my sudden shout to save it
Quick death beneath a pair of clogs.
'How can you bear to touch that thing,
So cold, so slimy?' I cradled it
Gently between my hands, and noticed
The body gleaming like new oil,
The still, green head, black buds of eyes,
That moon-terrain of camouflage
Quilting its back. But not for these kids

261

A matter of such sentiment:
Rather a sudden end like this,
Spiked on a fence, or crushed by a wheel,
Than any word which might betray
Their mapping of the old estate —
Tough, unyielding, not soft at all.
I carried it outside, and as I trudged
Towards the wettest, muddiest part,
Thought how easy it was to feel,
For once, so certain; then left it there
Carefully where the rushes grow,
Beside the dipping trees, the quiet stream,
In its own territory.

The Sweater

Christine, on her latest sweater, portrays
A pattern of lakes and rivers, mountains,
Two lambs at play in a grassy field
And, beneath a sky of blue,
A tiny house, a chimney smoking.

I do not know how my response
Is measured yet. But I am no traveller,
And landscapes such as this one, love,
Confuse, disorientate. Am I
Lost, perhaps, among the hills
On the journey home? Or, in my boat,
Stalled again between shore and shore,
Unable to reach you? And that house,
That house you built so carefully,
Was it I who lit the fire?

Paths

In the garden Daniel walks
The path's long tightrope to the hedge.
I stand beside the gate and watch,
Willing his steady progress to me, offering

My arms outstretched to guide him down
The last steep slope. But so much help
Is lost upon him here. He ducks his head
Defiantly away, his little brow
Tense now with his need to walk
The final steps alone. At the foot
Of the slope he pauses, turns to make
A new ascent, and I offer him
No barrier this time, only the love
I feel I owe, my wish for him
For gardens greener, paths
Much wider and more kind than this.

Nettles

They always grow wherever we are,
Or where we've been. To follow their progress
is to read a map to hidden places:
The gardens under clouds of bracken,
Run-down allotments, paths that run
From nowhere into nowhere, yet
Meant something once. Their roots sink down
Deep in nitrogen, erect
Markers for those who want to come
To strip the middens for their finds,
Or filter in the sombre fields
Traces of lost settlements.
But most ignore them till they grow
Too near a living house, for notice
How easily they take to ruins:
Masking fallen rubble, sealing
Entry at doors, windows, chimneys even;
Guarding in their silent way
better than those who've come and gone
The tenancies of earth and stone,
The privacies of all their lives.

R. S. Thomas

R.S. Thomas was born in Cardiff in 1913. He was rector of a number of Welsh parishes before his retirement to Llŷn and then Anglesey. Author of over twenty collections of verse, including *Collected Poems 1945-90* (Phoenix), he was recently nominated for the 1996 Nobel Prize for literature. These selections are from his Seren volume *Welsh Airs*. He is bilingual.

A Welshman at St. James's Park

I am invited to enter these gardens
As one of the public, and to conduct myself
In accordance with the regulations;
To keep off the grass and sample flowers
Without touching them; to admire birds
That have been seduced from wildness by
Bread they are pelted with.
                      I am not one
Of the public; I have come a long way
To realise it. Under the sun's
Feathers are the sinews of stone,
The curved claws.
                    I think of a Welsh hill
That is without fencing, and the men,
Bosworth blind, who left the heather
And the high pastures of the heart. I fumble
In the pocket's emptiness; my ticket
Was in two pieces. I kept half.

Fugue for Ann Griffiths

In which period
      do you get lost?
The roads lead
      under a twentieth century
sky to the peace
      of the nineteenth. There it is,
as she left it,
      too small to be chrysalis
of that clenched soul.
      Under the eaves the martins
continue her singing.
      Down this path she set off
for the earlier dancing
      of the body; but under the myrtle
the Bridegroom was waiting
      for her on her way home.

To put it differently
yet the same, listen,
friend:
      A nineteenth century calm;
that is, a countryside
      not fenced in
by cables and pylons,
but open to thought to blow in
      from as near as may be
to the truth.
            There were evenings
she would break it. See her
      at the dance, round
and round, hand
      in hand, weaving
invisible threads. When
you are young.... But
      there was One
with his eye on her;
      she saw him stand

under the branches.
                            History insists
on a marriage, but the husband was as cuckolded
as Joseph.
                    Listen again:

    To the knocker at the door:
    'Miss Thomas has gone dancing.'

    To the caller in time:
    'The mistress is sitting the dance

    out with God at her side.'
    To the traveller up learning's

    slope: 'She is ahead of you on her knees.
    She who had decomposed

    is composed again in her hymns.
    The dust settles on the Welsh language,

    but is blown away in great gusts
    week by week in chapel after chapel.'

Is there a scholarship that grows
naturally as the lichen? How
did she, a daughter of the land, come
by her learning? You have seen
her face, figure-head of a ship
outward bound? But she was not
alone: a trinity of persons
saw to it she kept on course
like one apprenticed since early
days to the difficulty of navigation
in rough seas. She described her turbulence
to her confessor, who was the more
astonished at the fathoms
of anguish over which she had
attained to the calmness of her harbours.

There are other pilgrimages
   to make beside Jerusalem, Rome;
beside the one into the no-man's-
   land beyond the microscope's carry.

If you came in winter,
   you would find the tree
with your belief still crucified
   upon it, that for her at all

times was in blossom, the resurrection
   of one that had come seminally
down to raise the deciduous human
   body to the condition of his body.

Hostilities were other peoples'.
Though a prisoner of the Lord
she was taken without fighting.

That was in the peace before
the wars that were to end
war. If there was a campaign

for her countrymen, it was one
against sin. Musically
they were conscripted to proclaim

Sunday after Sunday the year
round they were on God's side. England
meanwhile detected its enemies

from afar. These made friends
out in the fields because
of its halo with the ancestral scarecrow.

   Has she waited all these years
   for me to forget myself
   and do her homage? I begin
   now: Ann Thomas, Ann Griffiths,

one of a thousand Anns chosen
to confound your parentage
with your culture — I know
Powys, the leafy backwaters
it is easy for the spirit to forget
its destiny in and put on soil
for its crown. You walked solitary
there and were not tempted,
or took your temptation as calling
to see Christ rising in April
out of that same soil and clothing
his nakedness like a tree. Your similies
were agricultural and profound.
As winter is forgiven by spring's
blossom, so defoliated man,
thrusting his sick hand in the earth's
side is redeemed by conviction.
Ann, dear, what can our scholarship
do but wander like Efyrnwy
your grass library, wondering at the absence
of all volumes but one? The question
teases us like the undying
echo of an Amen high up
in the cumulus rafters over Dolanog.

       The theologians disagree
       on their priorities. For her
       the centuries' rhetoric contracted
       to the three-letter word. What was sin
       but the *felix culpa* enabling
       a daughter of the soil to move
       in divine circles? This was before
       the bomb, before the annihilation
       of six million Jews. It appears now
       the confession of a child before
       an upholstered knee; her achievement
       the sensitising of the Welsh
       conscience to the English rebuke.
       The contemporary miracle is the feeding

of the multitude on the sublime
mushroom, while the Jesus,
who was her lover, is a face
gathering moss on the gable
of a defunct chapel, a myth shifting
its place to the wrong end
of the spectrum under the Doppler
effect of the recession of our belief.

Three pilgrimages to Bardsey
equalling one to Rome — How close
need a shrine be to be too far
for the traveller of to-day who is in
a hurry? Spare an hour or two
for Dolanog — no stone cross,
no Holy Father. What question
has the country to ask, looking as if
nothing has happened since the earth
cooled? And what is your question?
She was young and was taken.
If one asked you: 'Are you glad
to have been born?' would you let
the positivist reply for you
by putting your car in gear, or watch
the exuberance of nature in a lost
village, that is life saying Amen
to itself? Here for a few years
the spirit sang on a bone bough
at eternity's window, the flesh trembling
at the splendour of a forgiveness
too impossible to believe in, yet believing.

Are the Amens over? Ann (*Gymraeg*)
you have gone now but left us with the question
that has a child's simplicity and a child's depth:
Does the one who called to you,

when the tree was green, call us
also, if with changed voice,

269

now the leaves have fallen and the boughs
are of plastic, to the same thing?

She listened to him.
We listen to her.
She was in time
chosen. We but infer
from the union of time
with space the possibility
of survival. She who was born
first must be overtaken
by our to-morrow.
So with wings pinned
and fuel rationed,
let us put on speed
to remain still
through the dark hours
in which prayer gathers
on the brow like dew,
where at dawn the footprints
of one who invisibly
but so close passed
discover a direction.

John Tripp

Born in 1927 in Bargoed, John Tripp worked as a journalist and Public Relations Officer in London before returning to Cardiff in the late sixties to work as a freelance writer. His untimely death in 1986 meant the loss of a lively and controversial voice. His *Selected Poems* edited by John Ormond, appeared in 1989.

The Diesel to Yesterday

There is downpour, always,
   as the carriages inch into Newport:
perhaps six times in ten years
   of a hundred visits to custom,
the entry to my country is uncurtained
   by rain or mist. I look
at the shambles of sidings and streets,
   the rust of progress and freight wagons,
the cracked facades of bingo cinemas.
   Sometimes I expect to see
the callous peaked caps and buttons
   of visa-checkers, cold sentries
on a foreign border, keeping out the bacillus
   in hammering rain and swirling fog.
Often I wish it were so, this frontier sealed
   at Chepstow, against frivolous incursion
from the tainting eastern zones.

Patience vanishes with frayed goodwill
   at the sight of the plump bundles
tumbling into Wales.

They bring only their banknotes
and a petrol-stenched lust for scenery
     to shut in their kodaks,
packing out the albums of Jersey
     and the anthill beaches of the south.
They stand in line for pre-heated grease
     in the slums of crumbled resorts,
nose their long cars into pastureland
     and the hearts of ancient townships
that now are buried under chromium plate.

I catch myself out in error, feel
     ignoble in disdain.
The bad smell at my nostril
     is some odour from myself —
A modern who reeks of the museum,
     not wanting his own closed yesterday
but the day before that,
     the lost day before dignity went,
when all our borders were sealed.

Matins

The flat blue days of summer
limp out, we wait for the russet carpets.
The last plane on the warm schedules
drops down to Rhoose, red lights flicking
from cockpit to tail. Friends behind glass guide them in.

               South of Bonvilston
I sit on an old brick wall and roll a smoke —
the knots of vivid faces recede
and with them, too, their warped testaments.

I sit on till daybreak there.
Milk churns stand by gates like sentries
as if abandoned from an earlier time;
the land flattens down to the shoreline,

thin rain stipples the inland ponds,
farm sheds askew on a tilt.
Not a juke-box, not a stockbroker, for miles.

Homage to Aneurin Bevan

The last time the silver cascaded for me
was at Brentford, of all places. He walked
between two awed local agents
who revelled in short glory
with this paramount trapper of hypocrites,
this Welsh word-weaver famed for his coup de grâce.

No one knew then, it was near the end,
he was sick even then as we heard
him lunge at the ones who could never grasp
his gospel, at the clever who could handle
brilliance for a minute in the chamber
when he stayed on facts,
but were lost when he purred in the venom,
whipped when he launched the tirades.

The slight lisp was still there as he thundered,
drumming up compassion for the poor, still
boxing with the governors to take drabness
out of ill-favoured lives,
lifting his hand as if to snuff out a candle,
shocking us again with the unmatched wit,
the logic clear as glass.

It is easy to be brave in company, linking hands,
but this one was out on the ramparts, night after night,
alone. And when he disappeared,
a portcullis slammed down,
leaving the captain of archers outside.

End of a Farrier

The gangs of Irish in their huge boots
get up early. They have come here today
to destroy my father's forge.
Inside there is still the reek of burned hoof,
the rusted anvil is in the weed
with the punctured bellows. Dozers ram
the wood walls, the tin roof collapses
in a hung fog of black dust.

Hard on the slide-rule, the cranes swing and dip
hooking this shop of old craft off the map,
cleaving a furrow for the fast truck, Ford and Jaguar.
Here once the children stood for hours
wide-eyed at the hunter's kick, shod pony, shire
and the stunning palomino. Deep-voiced women
slid from expensive saddles, and men in pink
shared a flask before the blood hunt.

It is raining, but the Irish don't stop.
There's good money in wrecking
and the porter taps never run dry.

My father is handed a cheque
from the man in the bowler and grey suit.
He is now out to grass himself,
silently plotting to pack his gaping calendar.
We walk home in the rain,
away from forty years of his life.

Castle

On the tour the old guide showed us
the great banqueting hall where they feasted
off huge chops, swan, venison, brandy wine;
and the bedrooms where they enjoyed incest,
breeding simpletons to keep it in the family

and a name on the enormous maps.
  A priest was kept at the back
  on a pallet and ration of wine
  to bless killers off to Jerusalem.

Then we saw the dungeons' slimed walls
with rack, screws, brazier and rusted manacles
where they cut off tongues and put out eyes.
  When kings held a Christmas court,
the baying of hounds and the squawking of chickens
blotted out the screams from downstairs.

It was all log-fires then —
wood, stone, leather, hide and sheepskin
in turrets of fatal draught, the women tough as boots
through marriages of freezing utility.

The guide didn't mention the smells and disease,
or the rats, the battalions of cockroaches.
  Or the intelligence
of corkscrew lords, devious in the bone.
Or the dark and endless boredom
when those lovely, tall, fat, twelve-day candles
                    red-numeral-marked in sections
                    night by night sank into their wax....

John Powell Ward

John Powell Ward was born in Suffolk in 1937 and educated at the Universities of Toronto, Cambridge and Wales. A lecturer at UCW Swansea for many years, he is the author of *The Poetry of R.S. Thomas* among other works and is currently the editor of Seren's *BorderLines* series. His new Seren collection is *Genesis*.

London Welsh v. Bridgend

Then I got on the train, very late
at night, Saturday, and lay on the seat,
exhausted, as did the other man
there, a little man, beady-eyed and
with a pointed chin, and he pulled the
blinds down, and we lay, and just about
dozed off when bam! door opened,
in came half a rugby team, enormous
fellows, tipped me off the seat on the
filthy floor, then sat down, singing,
shouting, crashing on each other with
their beer cans, and one sat by the
beady man, running his fingers exquisitely
along the fellow's thigh-bone, through
his trousers, but in only a bawdy
way, friendly even, if you could believe
it, and they roughed, and one
arse in the corridor, undid the fire
extinguisher, soaked us, and another
slammed the door, sat down again, kept
asking me the beady man's name, which

I didn't know, angry now, afraid even,
but decided to be sensible, and got
going, talked, had their beer, and they
got serious to meet me, a most
generous gesture, and a big man, older
than the others, kept deflecting the
attention, of the bawdy one from the
beady one, the bawdy one trying to make
the beady one talk, which he couldn't,
in inhibition, and cringing fear, and I
felt sorry, but leant on the carriage arm,
with them, drinking, singing, yawning, and
hearing about his wife, from one of them,
till, at last, they were quieter, they had
won their match, they had had a good day,
and they dozed off, one on my shoulder, sixteen
stone, snoring loudly, but I finally dozed
off, at the train's rhythm, rattling
through the darkness, and I half-woke,
at times, saw a misty scene, as of Arthur's
knights, assembled, swaying, brief white
faces, then dozed, felt the train stop
in my half-asleep condition, and men get
out, a shrieking porter, and banging doors,
then slept again, and then woke, two
hundred miles from London, they had
all gone, every one, bar the beady one, and I
sat, heavy, soggy, wanting lukewarm tea, and
saw, with my round eye and my mind's eye,
the aftermath of dawn, and the mess of the
twentieth century; the industry, the steel
works and the smelting works, a new day, for
better or for worse in our hands, and the
carriage window, filthy, but a filter,
for that streaky, watery, nearly
light-blue, blue.

Dreaming Birds

The eyes and feathers intermesh.
Descartes said birds were small machines.
A startled starling clattered off
And flew away at that, it screeched
That birds are loops in modern minds,
Weird flights, a mode, a fatal curve
Of values in the air. The thrush

Is proto-sculpture on the lawn,
The SS crow patrolling down
A motorway's hard shoulder struts
At sentry duty. From a pole
A blackbird soloist transmits
Its live performance and the cool
Woods pay to hear him, dark guitars

Are slung there and electric cries
Flash down the alleyways of spruce,
Afforestation's gentlest crop.
The dreamer Kant thought of a dove
That found air fretful and conceived
A purer flight in empty space.
I dream of swifts and soar asleep.

Elegiac

Seals die sad-eyed, whales writhe, fish found dead.
Species mysteriously disappear. Butterflies
Slip away, elephants and rhinos murdered.
Survivors are vermin and beautiful insects.

The atmosphere punctured like stretched rubber.
The forests wither, the lakes burst into flame.
The fuel that pampers us rainbows the air.
The dune beaches are boxed with hotels.

Yobs mob with their broken bottles, admired.
Yacht havens lilt rather softly on oil.
Yellow white black seethe loudly, too openly.
Years at a time drift, faster and faster.

Lying on the moon are a few footprints
Likely to stay exactly so for ever.
Love is a medium, a territory, an air.
Life shifts sideways, by inches in the mind.

Enormous changes are upon us, friend.
Education, the marvellous chance, was rejected.
Euthanasia an urgent and dangerous option.
Electricity, nature's last breath and pulse.

In The Box

Father, I have sinned and I confess.
For I am white, male and middle-class and

Was brought up in the south-east of England.
Wretched I turn desperately to you asking what

To do with these appalling errors. I have
Tried living in Canada five years and (oh shame,

Shame) in Wales twenty-five, running a cockney
Stepney youth club, stopping my offspring

(Both male too god forgive me) from yuppie-talk and
Bringing home their ghastly Oxbridge friends, I

Even give a percentage to selected charities.
Every day I deprave myself just the same,

And now know not where to turn. The worst
Aspect is this nauseating guilt-complex which

279

Makes me ape people's accents, pretend to like
Music-murder on the streets and all the time

Really just avoiding women, patronizing blacks and
Releasing aggro on youth and equals. God, it festers,

Old plants lose their blossoms (OK like men
Other parts, which in my case don't reach I

Guess), they turn brown and a nasty smell and die.
God. God. Did I really think all those Tory things

In those earlier years, and am stuck with them as
If no good feeling, no love, ever moved me? I come to

You for forgiveness, yes, but for guidance too in my
Years left such as may be granted. The millennium

Comes nearer, the planet's population groups realign
Casually, cautiously and creatively, and old material

Declines as it should and must. Forgive my reactionary
Demeanour; it is a mere stuck groove and a worn

Lazy failure to rotate on the poor axis of flesh.
Life, as always, goes. I've had mine. Forgive, father.

A Maybe Epitaph

Hung like a spotlight in the dark
Huddles our reconstructed park.
Hopes revamping down from dreams.
How perfunctory it seems.

Earth contracts, each target place
Enters a final dose of space.
Extra gendering the test.
Every remaining grief expressed.

Scientists researching find
Something various in the mind
Sufficient for each probity.
Saviour dolphin, friendly tree.

Twist the roses from the light.
Time the crops to radiate.
Thank you speakers, never wrong.
Thank you singing, for your song.

Allocate what water's left,
Add survival's havering gift.
After noon the cosmic term,
Ash and swirl and nanotime.

Frances Williams

Frances Williams was born in Bridgend in 1968. She won the Cardiff Literature Festival's Young Writers' Competition in 1986 and her collection of poems, *Flotsam*, was published by Seren in 1988. She studied art in Liverpool before completing an MA in sculpture in London. She is currently editor of the national lesbian magazine, *Diva*.

Space

Through my clouded breath I
See the constellations hang; pink

Venus wavers beneath the
Tilt of Cassiopeia's chair, and Orion hints

Of coincidence, his sword the three of a black dice
Slung, waiting to be read. As if a saucepan

Tossed stars up, the Plough also
Waits, ready to catch a fall. But

Nothing moves. Except satellite's clockwork
Pace, shifting like a compass point

Plotting an arc, and jet's red
Landing lights that blink — all

Mechanics amongst the stillness of such glitter.
Ancient or modern, names and fables make

No sense of this. Only to feel vastness
Creep to the corners of your eye, and the wait
For something to reveal itself.

The Plum Tree

Where the top twigs reach
Amongst the green calligraphy of leaf,
Plums droop. All the colours of bruises,
Blue dust and purple, they're
Fleshy to the pip. Here wasps

Rip through air in a hurricane
Frenzy of black and yellow, maddened
By a succulence so fat, plums
Burst their skins and bleed. Sun
Roasts them deep, warm as sunburnt

Flesh. They move through every
Stage of death; most rot where they
Hang, stippled with fungus. This slipping
From ripeness to decay persists,
Regardless of the effort

Unfulfilled; a faith in the future's
Goodness that never fails
But each year overspills.

Splott

A grid of terraces, domino
Lined, broken by warehouses,
Brick churches, paint peeled halls.

This part of town, distinguished
Only by its roughness. Around here,
Even the dogs are streetwise, a cocky

Spring in their mongrel loins.
Slabs of offices behind, stoop
Over the web of streets, keeping
Watch of their small offspring, casting

Long shadows. There's barking
In the alleyways as sun falls
Behind the black nests of chimneypots,
Lighting like furnaces the tall towers.

The Fog Horn

In this soup thick night, the fog horn
Calls, like a cow in pain
Sounding its lonely rhythms. Its long

Notes travel not only the sea's swell, but
Float over fields full of sleeping cattle, then

To towns, through deserted streets,
Pulsing through my window, reaching

My ears. How many people listen,
Lying in their soft beds awake
To the soft displacement of silence.

Like hearing a dying animal,
It proves that yet a life exists
Marking the human shorelines
With its pulse.

And all around the sea
Stretches, falling over the horizon's rims.

SOURCES

All of the following titles have been published by Seren/Poetry Wales Press.

Bryan Aspden: 'News of the Changes' is the title poem from *News of the Changes* (1984). 'Dragons', 'A Rum Game' and 'Erw Fawr' are all from *Blind Man's Meal* (1988).

Barbara Bentley: all of the poems are from *Living Next to Leda* (1996).

Ruth Bidgood: 'Kindred', 'Edward Bach Advises His Sister', 'Lichen, 'Cladonia Fimbriata', 'Sheep in the Hedge', 'Stateless', 'Tourists', 'Spiders', 'Emu's Egg' and 'Earth Tremor' are collected in *Selected Poems* (1992). 'Blue Tit Feeding' is from *The Fluent Moment* (1996).

Stewart Brown: 'Glad Rags', 'Springs and Balances', 'Calabash Carver, Chaffe' are from *Zinder* (1986). 'Was-Beetle' and 'Alphobiabet' are from *Lugard's Bridge* (1989).

Duncan Bush: 'Nausea' and 'The Sunflower' are from *Aquarium* (1983). 'Pneumoconiosis' and 'Hill Farmer, Staring into his Fire' are from *Salt* (1985). 'Living in Real Times', 'Brigitte Bardot in Grangetown', 'A.I.D.S. (The Movie)', 'The Sunday the Power Went Off' and 'Just a Few Things Daddy Knows About Ice' are from *Masks* (1994). Duncan Bush is also the author of *The Genre of Silence*, a book-length work featuring poems and prose.

Vuyelwa Carlin: 'The Topiarist', 'Lais at Corinth', 'Medusa Feeds her Pets' and 'Elisabeth I' are from *Midas' Daughter* (1991). 'Alfred's Childhood Journey to Rome' and 'The Books' are from *How We Dream of the Dead* (1995).

Tony Conran: all of the poems are from *Blodeuwedd* (1988).

Eleanor Cooke: all of the poems are from *A Kind of Memory* (1988).

Tony Curtis: 'The Death of Richard Beattie-Seaman in the Belgian Grand Prix, 1939', 'Soup', 'Portrait of the Painter Hans Theo Richter and his wife Gisela in Dresden, 1933 — Otto Dix' and 'Incident on a Hospital Train from Calcutta, 1944' are collected in *War Voices* (1995). 'Swimming Class', 'Ivy' and 'My Father' are collected in *Selected Poems* (1986). 'Breaking Surface' and 'Making Bread for *Sunblest*' are in *Last Candles* (1989). 'Taken for Pearls' and 'Coracle' are from *Taken for Pearls* (1993).

John Davies: 'In Port Talbot', 'Border Incident' and 'Five Canoes' are from *The Visitor's Book* (1985). 'How to Write Anglo-Welsh Poetry' appears in *Anglo-Welsh Poetry 1480-1990* edited by Raymond Garlick and Roland Mathias. 'Barry John', 'Howard', 'Things to do when the town's closed' and 'Bards' are from *Flight Patterns* (1991).

Jean Earle: 'Jugged Hare', 'In the Night', 'Honesty', 'Afterwards', 'Static' and 'Stillborn' are collected in Jean Earle's *Selected Poems* (1990). 'Wife and Dolphin' first appeared in *Visiting Light* (1987). 'Gran and Gramp at the Fireworks' and 'Your Aura' are from *The Sun in the West* (1995).

Christine Evans: 'Callers', 'Summer in the Village', 'Exchange' and 'First Lamb' are from *Looking Inland* (1983). 'Knife' and 'Lucy's Bones' are in *Cometary Phases* (1989). 'Morning Watch', 'Case History' and 'On Retreat' are from *Island of Dark Horses* (1995). Christine Evans is also the author of the book-length poem, *Falling Back* (1986).

Peter Finch: 'A Welsh Wordscape', 'The Tattoo', and 'Putting Kingsley Amis in the Microwave' are collected in *Selected Poems* (1987). 'Winners', 'Kipper on the Lips', 'Ex-Smokes Man Writes Epic' and 'Severn Estuary ABC' are from *Poems for Ghosts* (1991).

Catherine Fisher: 'Immrama', 'Snake-bite', 'Severn Bore' and 'St. Tewdric's Well' are from *Immrama* (1988). 'On the Third Day', 'Tapestry Room', 'Incident at Conwy' and 'In a Chained Library' are from *The Unexplored Ocean* (1994).

Rose Flint: all of the poems are from *Blue Horse of Morning* (1991).

Desmond Graham: the 'Character' poems are from *The Lie of Horizons* (1993). 'At the Municipal Cemetery, Gdynia' and 'For Milena' are in *The Marching Bands* (1996).

Steve Griffiths: 'Courage', 'Small substantial shadow' and 'Llantysilio, overgrown' were in *Civilised Airs* (1984). 'Glyndŵr Subdued' is from *Uncontrollable Fields (1993)*. 'The Mines in sepia tint', 'Llangefni Market', 'Taking Shelter', 'Fluidity, Charmouth' and all of the poems above have been collected in *Selected Poems* (1993).

Paul Groves: 'All Hallows' Eve', 'Anniversary Soak', 'Forgetting Water' and 'Greta Garbo' feature in *Academe* (1988). 'The Back End of the Horse', 'Eduardo on a Scooter', 'The Torturer's Coffee' and 'Ultima Thule' are from *Ménage à Trois* (1995).

Mike Haines: both of the poems are from *Seeds of Things* (1985).

Paul Henry: 'Widows of Talyllyn', 'Trevor's', 'Busker' and 'Museum Café' are from Paul Henry's *Time Pieces* (1993). 'Comins Coch', 'Fatherless Friends', and 'At This Hour' are from *Captive Audience* (1996).

Joyce Herbert: all of the poems are from *Approaching Snow* (1983).

Lucien Jenkins: all of the poems are from *Laying Out The Body* (1992).

Mike Jenkins: 'Chartist Meeting' and 'A Truant' are from *The Common Land* (1981). 'Reflection in a Reservoir' and 'Memorials' are in *Empire of Smoke* (1983). 'Industrial Museum' and 'Canine Graffiti' are from *Invisible Times* (1986). 'Creature' is in *A Dissident Voice* (1990). 'Famous Player' and 'Gurnos Shops' are from *This House, My Ghetto* (1995).

Nigel Jenkins: all of the poems are from *Song and Dance* (1981).

Kate Johnson: all of the poems are from *Gods* (1987).

Glyn Jones: 'Esyllt', 'Watcher', 'The Seagull', 'Dawn Trees', "The Common Path' and 'Remembering Siani' are collected in *Selected Poems: Fragments & Fictions* (1988). Acknowledgements are due to the Estate of Glyn Jones for permission to reprint.

Sally Roberts Jones: all of the poems are from *Relative Values* (1985).

Peter Thabit Jones: all of the poems are from *Visitors* (1986).

Tim Liardet: 'Summer Storm' and 'Under Upper Tier' are from *Clay Hill* (1988). 'Palimpsest for a Radio Play', 'Fellini Beach' and 'Hart Crane on *The Orizaba*' are from *Fellini Beach* (1994).

Hilary Llewellyn-Williams: 'Holly', 'Breadmaking' and 'The Trespasser' are from *The Tree Calendar* (1987). 'Feeding the Bat', 'Brynberllan', 'The Sealwife' and 'Andarax' are from *Book of Shadows* (1990).

Christopher Meredith: all of the poems are in *Snaring Heaven* (1990).

Kathy Miles: all of the poems are from *The Rocking-Stone* (1988).

Robert Minhinnick: 'Driving in Fog' and 'Rhys' are from *Life Sentences* (1983). 'Big Pit, Blaenafon', 'On the Llŷn Fawr Hoard in the National Museum of Wales' and 'Eelers' are in *The Dinosaur Park* (1985). 'The Looters' is the title poem from the volume of that name (1989). 'Hey Fatman' and 'World War II comes to XXI Heol Eglwys' are from *Hey Fatman* (1994).

Leslie Norris: all of the poems are from *Collected Poems* (1986).

John Ormond: all of the selections are in *Selected Poems* (1987). Thanks are due to his Estate for permission to reprint.

Gwyn Parry: 'His Graveyard', 'Miner's Candles' and 'June' are from *The Hurricane* (1987). 'Mynydd Parys' is the title poem of the volume of that name (with photographs by Steve Makin) (1990).

Richard Poole: all of the poems are in *Words Before Midnight* (1981).

Sheenagh Pugh: 'Sometimes' and 'She was nineteen, and she was bored' are from *Beware Falling Tortoises* (1987). Those poems and 'Spring '72', 'The Black Beach' and 'Do you think we'll ever get to see earth, sir?' are collected in her *Selected Poems* (1990). 'Remember, Remember' is from *Sing for the Taxman* (1993). 'The Embarkation of the Pigs' will appear in her forthcoming collection *ID'S HOSPIT*.

Deryn Rees-Jones: all of the poems are from *The Memory Tray* (1994).

Don Rodgers: all of the poems are from *Moontan* (1996).

Frances Sackett: all of the poems are from *The Hand Glass* (1996).

287

Graham Thomas: all of the poems are from *The One Place* (1983).

R.S. Thomas: 'A Welshman in St. James's Park' and 'Fugue for Ann Griffiths' are in *Welsh Airs* (1987). Seren has also published another collection by Thomas, *Ingrowing Thoughts* (1985).

John Tripp: all of the poems are collected in *Selected Poems* (ed. John Ormond, 1989). Thanks are due to his Estate for permission to reprint..

John Powell Ward: 'London Welsh v. Bridgend' appears in *To Get Clear* (1981). 'Dreaming Birds' is from *The Clearing* (1984). 'Elegiac' and 'In The Box' are from *A Certain Marvellous Thing* (1993). 'A Maybe Epitaph' is from *Genesis* (1996).

Frances Williams: all of the poems are from *Flotsam* (1987).

The Editor

Born in Florida, U.S.A., Amy Wack was educated at San Diego State and Columbia Universities. She has been the Poetry Editor for Seren books since 1992, and is also the Reviews Editor for *Poetry Wales* magazine. She lives in Cardiff with her husband and daughter.